FUGITIVE SON

FUGITIVE

SON

A MEMOIR

ARAMÍS

CALDERÓN

POTOMAC BOOKS

AN IMPRINT OF THE UNIVERSITY OF NEBRASKA PRESS

Library of Congress Cataloging-in-Publication Data
Names: Calderón, Aramís, author.
Title: Fugitive son: a memoir / Aramís Calderón.
Description: [Lincoln]: Potomac Books, an imprint
of the University of Nebraska Press, [2024]
Identifiers: LCCN 2024008369
ISBN 9781640126268 (paperback)
ISBN 9781640126336 (epub)
ISBN 9781640126343 (pdf)
Subjects: LCSH: Calderón, Aramís. | Children
of criminals. | Fugitives from justice. | BISAC:
BIOGRAPHY & AUTOBIOGRAPHY / Military
Classification: LCC HV6251 .C35 2024 | DDC
364.3092 [B]—dc23/eng/20240601
LC record available at https://lccn.loc.gov/2024008369

Designed and set in Janson Text by N. Putens.

For my father and his grandchildren

ACKNOWLEDGMENTS

Writing is a solitary activity, and yet it's a team sport. This book owes a great deal to Jeff Hess, my writing mentor and leader of the DD-214 Writers' Workshop, for his no-nonsense advice and encouragement. I'd also like to thank my early readers and the members of the workshop for their feedback: Libby Oberg, Jonathan Tennis, Tom Morrison, Dr. Bill Monaco, and Tim Wright.

I'm grateful to my agent, Tracy Crow, for her patience and hard work in finding a home for this book. I first met Tracy years ago by way of reading her craft book, *On Point: A Guide to Writing the Military Story*. It was the first book about writing I had ever read, and it directly helped set me on the path of becoming a writer. I hereby thank you even more for writing that book.

To my wife, best friend, and the owner of my favorite bookstore, Portkey Books, Crystel Gail Calderón, thank you for holding me together while I tore myself apart to find the words tied to my most painful memories. To my children Arabelle, Ilyana, and Lysander: I am happy you are part of this world.

Finally, for the shadow in my heart. I don't think my father deserves thanks for this book, but I wouldn't have this life and my children if I hadn't been his son.

A NOTE ON TRANSLATION

I witnessed the difficulties of Arabic transliteration while reading intelligence reports during my deployments to Iraq. For example, I came across thirty-six different spellings of Muhammad, and I know there to be even more. My father and I weren't native speakers, and moreover there's no universally accepted transliteration of Arabic. So for the sake of consistency, I kept my father's Arabic spelling and hyphens.

FUGITIVE SON

1

We spent our summer Sundays visiting my father in prison.

To be closer to him, my mother had moved us from Florida to Baton Rouge, Louisiana, when I was eleven. The long, one-lane road from our apartment to the prison was flanked by swamp, and the stink of an unseen petrochemical plant filled the car even when the windows were rolled up. To pass the time, Mom would crank up the radio volume and sing along to Whitney Houston and Bryan Adams songs about love and loneliness. My siblings napped, and I'd pass the time reading a map we kept stored in the glove box. Our destination on the map was a town named Carville.

On August 16, 1992, we were running late as usual. Mom parked in the visitors' area, a gravel lot with a view of the Mississippi River just beyond a barbed wire fence. She tried walking quickly through the parking lot, but her high heels sank into the ground every other step. I held my little brother's hand, but Peewee's little legs struggled to keep up. My sisters, Memé and Chiní, skipped and laughed, happy to be out of the car. As soon as Mom's heels hit the sidewalk, she took off even faster. I couldn't understand why. Even the few times we'd been late for visitation hours, Dad's anger had dropped after a hug and a kiss.

The federal corrections facility housed minimum-security inmates with medical conditions. Mom had said they moved Dad here because of his bad knees. Next door to the prison was a leper colony, but I never saw any of the residents.

I knew back then my father had committed crimes, but I didn't understand what "conspiracy drug trafficking" meant. I knew he was a drug smuggler, and I knew what the word *smuggler* meant because Han Solo in the movie *Star Wars* was also one. Teachers had taught me drugs were bad, but I'd learned that lesson long before the D.A.R.E. program appeared in my school. Still, I didn't believe my dad was a bad man.

A garden surrounded the prison. The able-bodied inmates planted and maintained a riot of manicured bushes punctuated with bright red and yellow flowers. The guards were polite and happy, unlike the rough-spoken corrections officers with their thin-lipped smiles whom I remembered from Dad's previous prison stay, at the maximum-security Homestead Correctional Institution in Florida.

The reception area was in a rectangular white concrete building that always reminded me of a shoebox. We followed Mom through the heavy door with its thick glass pane. I was out of breath and felt the stab of a stitch under my ribcage. Little brother Peewee's face was covered with sweat. Mom checked us in with the guard, and he thanked her and called her "ma'am." She shooed us over to the waiting area, and we occupied ourselves among the other kids. Peewee and I stayed away from the boys and my sisters from the girls.

The family waiting area was the best I'd ever seen. The moms here sat a little straighter, and the kids smiled more. Toys for the visiting kids were clean. The Barbie dolls my sisters played with had their heads and all their limbs, and the board games were complete. Here, the guards announced the start of visiting hours in soft voices, and they didn't search adults for contraband. Mom sat in a chair with a clean, cushioned seat and read a beauty magazine with Julia Roberts on the cover. After seeing the movie *Pretty Woman*, my mother had adopted a hairstyle to resemble her. She'd even dyed her hair red.

The inmate visitation area provided large plastic picnic tables and clear views into the garden. My father sat alone at one of the tables. In the other prisons he would pass the time waiting for us by talking with the other inmates, but here, no one even looked at him. Dad didn't seem to care. I assumed the inmates feared him.

When Dad caught sight of us that day, he waved us over. His tan jumpsuit was a size too large. We hugged him all at the same time, and he embraced us all within his arms. I saw his prisoner number stenciled in black block characters on his back: 39941-019.

Dad said, "As-salamu-aliakum."

We replied in a chorus of broken Arabic, "Wa-aliakum-salam."

His cheeks turned pink when he smiled at us, his trimmed goatee framing his lips. "Good. Your pronunciation is getting better." I avoided all the eyes on us every time we spoke Arabic to each other.

Dad practiced Islam, that of the Shia sect to be exact. Like most Argentinians, he had been raised in the Catholic Church. Whenever I asked him why he'd converted, he'd tell me that Christian doctrines hadn't appealed to him, and the sense of guilt and shame in the Christian creed reeked to his soul of hypocrisy. He'd repeat the story of how he'd become functionally godless during his teenage years, until he'd converted to Islam in the 1970s during his first stint doing hard time in the U.S. federal prison system; there, he said he'd befriended a good Muslim man, who mentored my father and protected him. I understood later, through my own wartime experiences in Iraq, that there were no atheists in foxholes.

Mom repeated the Arabic greeting like a robot. My father had converted her after they'd met. She, too, was a disillusioned Catholic, but at best she was an unenthusiastic Muslim woman. I never saw her wear a hijab, and she only prayed with Dad.

By Islamic laws and my father's insistence, we kids were all Muslims. All of us had Islamic middle names, proclaimed we were Muslim, and even avoided eating pork to make Dad happy.

I sat across from Dad, while Mom and Memé sat beside him. Chiní and Peewee sat next to me. Dad kissed Mom, tongue and everything, and my siblings and I made a chorus of disgusted disapproval.

When they finished, Dad looked each of us in the eyes. "You all look healthy." He looked at me a second time. "Are you swimming or doing exercises, Peté?"

We all had nicknames in my family, and they rarely called me Aramís. I hadn't even known my name was Aramís until the second grade, when I cried because my teacher yelled at me for not responding to daily attendance. When I was a baby, I had a large pacifier, and in Spanish it's called a *chupeté*, and ever since they've called me Peté.

"Yeah, there's a pool in the apartment complex." The week before, I had walked back home under the summer sun and burned the bottoms of my feet.

He turned to Mom. "Lele, stop buying that sugary cereal." Mom sighed and waved away his critique. "Leave him alone, Evaristo." She usually called him Eva and only used his full given name when something was wrong and she needed his attention.

I didn't understand what Dad was getting at. The only emotion my eleven-year-old mind registered was happiness at seeing him. He shook his head and turned to kiss Memé's head.

Dad peered under the table and pointed at the knock-off Converse footwear my grandma had bought me at Payless. "You need to get boots, Peté. Those sneakers provide no support." He took the welfare of my feet seriously and always told me how boots, preferably combat boots, were better for me and my size.

Mom interrupted Dad before he could remind me how, if I didn't take care of my feet, I would be dead in a war. "Evaristo, we need to talk." She'd used his full name again. They held each other's gaze.

"No." Memé wrapped her chubby arms around Dad. After Dad

gave a halfhearted attempt to break free, he smiled and licked her forehead. She giggled and let go.

Dad wiped her hair back and pointed with his chin to a door. "Go play together in the garden. There are butterflies there." He blew a kiss at my baby sister. "Do you like butterflies, Chiní?"

Chiní got up and headed toward the door. Dad reached across the table and squeezed my hand. "Don't let your five-year-old sister go out there alone. And take your brother." He barked the words like an order given to me by a military superior.

I never enjoyed being commanded by him, but I obeyed with protest. "How come Memé gets to stay?" Memé and I were only a year apart and afflicted with severe sibling rivalry.

Dad scoffed, "She's not." He kissed her and nudged her with his shoulder. She rose from his side and hopped to my side. "You take care of her too." Again, he commanded. Memé smiled because he'd raised his voice at me. One more point went to her in our endless game of who was the favorite.

The temperature outside had risen fast. The month of August in Baton Rouge was just as muggy and hot as in Miami, but there was no ocean breeze here. We played outside but again segregated by gender. Peewee and I played hide-and-seek, but we got bored and eventually I coaxed him to follow me and throw twigs at our sisters. Memé retaliated with rocks, but a stern look from a corrections officer ended the game.

We wandered the garden with all the other children of convicts, but we never spoke to one another. I believed each convict's kid had been conditioned by our lives to be suspicious of our own kind. I know now we were merely ashamed.

A butterfly as big as my face flew near me. I'd never seen one that big before. I didn't see the beauty of its wings or the grace of its flight; instead, I heard the wind whooshing under its wings and the spindly, predator-like legs. It sent me into a panic. I used every curse word I'd learned from the school bus and at home. It felt like thousands of them were crawling all over, trying to enter my ears and into my brain. I ran back inside to my mother.

My father had his arms around Mom. She wasn't leaning into him, and neither was smiling, but I had more pressing concerns. Behind me Memé was laughing.

I sat down and buried my face into my arms, covering my ears. Dad tapped the table with his knuckles. "What's going on, Peté?"

Before I could get my shit together, Memé told him how I'd run from a pretty butterfly, she said, "like a pussy."

"What? You ran away and left your little brother and sisters?" Dad grabbed my wrist, not unkindly but not softly. "Answer me."

I was more scared of the butterfly than his disappointment at that moment, and yet if I spoke, I knew my voice would crack. Dad despised men who cried, so I kept quiet.

"Leave him alone," Mom said, without sympathy or kindness.

"No." Dad got up slowly. "We're going to conquer this right now. Let's go, soldier." He staggered the first few steps and then found a more dignified stride the closer he got to the garden door. Both his knees had been broken when the cocaine-loaded plane he was flying crashed into the Caribbean Sea. His right leg was shorter than the other, and the skin around his knees was covered in scar tissue.

I followed him out the door back to the garden, my siblings and mother behind me. Memé ran forward and grabbed Dad's hand and led him to the monster butterfly.

It didn't seem as frightening to me at a distance, but I still stayed as far away as I could. Dad reached out to the butterfly, and it crawled up his hand. "This is beautiful. Al-humdu Allah, truly a marvel of His creation. Come see, Peté."

I didn't step up. My siblings got close to it, Memé and Chiní touching its wings with their fingertips and Peewee laughing as it slowly crawled around Dad's hand. My father stepped closer to me, and Mom stood behind me to keep me from running.

It was beautiful and terrifying.

"This is a harmless creature." Dad extended his hand to me.

I leaned as far from it as I could. "How do you know?"

The butterfly's wings rose and fell slowly. "Peté, the only thing you fear is fear itself." He gestured for me to give him my hand.

I looked away. The corrections officers and families glanced in our direction but ignored us when they saw who was talking. There was nothing to see here but a hardened criminal teaching his son to not be afraid of butterflies.

He lowered his voice. "Look at it."

I shook my head. Before Dad could try again with platitudes, the butterfly grew bored of my cowardice and flew off.

Dad's sigh rumbled like the gravel rocks Mom struggled to walk over every time we visited him. "Peté." He gripped my shoulder. "Son, that was a chance right there to confront and overcome your fears. You can't run away from your fears, or they will own you."

I remained silent. He would ignore my rationalizations about poisonous varieties and how vulnerable the inner ear was. I knew my words were mere excuses coming to him from his disappointment of a son anyway. His first arrest was at twelve years old. By sixteen he was a father and a cocaine cowboy by eighteen; no satisfactory explanation of my fears existed. He shook his head and turned away.

We walked back together to the table indoors. My sisters spent the rest of the visit telling Dad about their new schools, while Peewee sat on his lap and leaned against his shoulder.

Mom looked bored and chewed her nails. Whatever she and Dad had been talking about before wasn't so important anymore.

Dad didn't speak to me for the rest of the visit until he said in parting, "As-salamu-aliakum."

We lived on the second story of a working-class apartment complex in Baton Rouge where single moms and grandmothers raised families. We didn't visit my father the next weekend, so I spent the afternoons fishing and at night watched *Star Trek* reruns. One school night, we went to bed late after a dinner of store-brand macaroni and cheese. My brother, two sisters, and I slept in a heap in our mother's room to feel safe. Not every night, but often. Her bed was a double mattress on the floor. Like everything we had, our furniture was a collection of hand-me-downs and Salvation Army donations. Memé slept on the bed with Mom, Peewee on the other side of her. Chiní slept on the floor next to him. I lay at my mother's feet.

Monday morning, after midnight but before sunrise, a loud crash woke us. I felt it in my chest. Mom and my siblings clutched each other, gibbering and asking questions in the dark.

Mom called to me. Instead of running to her side, I remained in my sheets and pretended to be asleep. I wanted to melt down into the shallow-pile carpet.

I thought someone had made a mistake. We had nothing worth stealing, nothing of value in a two-bedroom, one-bath apartment with a family of five. Our most expensive appliance, the TV, was cheap.

When I didn't make a move, Memé separated herself from Mom and peeked into the hallway outside the bedroom.

A man in full body armor like a G.I. Joe action figure barked a command: "Hands in the air!"

I stopped pretending to sleep.

He pointed his semiautomatic rifle straight at my sister's chest. Memé froze. My mother screamed.

The intruders weren't burglars; it was the cops. Later I learned it wasn't SWAT or some other tactical law enforcement unit; they were federal marshals.

The feds didn't fire on my sister.

There is a hole in my memory. I don't know what happened after that moment. There is nothing there. I have looked. It is possible I kept my eyes closed the whole time and played dead. Fear owned me.

Once, years before, Mom had told me about being a little girl amid the gun battles in the streets of Havana, Cuba, during the communist revolution. She had hallucinated everyone's heads were small, like the size of a doll's head. I learned this was how some children processed the trauma of war—the mind distorting vision in response to the panic and fear induced by the combat. It is possible my mind protected me by ceasing to record my consciousness as soon as I saw the M16s.

I hated those feds for a long time. My forgiveness didn't come until I committed the same act on others. It was a difficult thing to reconcile with: ten years after this violation of my home I would do the same thing those men in armor did, only to another vulnerable family—in Iraq.

Like me, they were poor, desperate, afraid, and completely powerless.

Like me, those little children didn't deserve to have their home invaded.

I wonder if those lawmen hesitated just like I did when I saw those young and dirty faces.

All I do know of that moment in our apartment is that the feds questioned Mom, but she had no information, and they had no cause to take her into custody. They left us and walked out through the door they had ruined.

The sun rose, and my stream of consciousness resumed recording.

Chiní and Peewee went back to our room. Memé and I sat next to Mom on our couch. I asked Mom, "Why did this happen?"

Mom's face was swollen from crying. She said, "Dad escaped. The feds came looking for him." She smiled. Her teeth were crooked and stained. Her fear of dentists prevented us from seeing one.

I tried to speak but never finished a sentence. It was difficult to comprehend that he had escaped. I wanted to know why he didn't come for us before the feds did. My head felt stuffed with carpet fuzz. I was tired. Memé had dried tears on her cheeks.

Outside, children were laughing and playing. Mom said, "It's a school day. Get ready for school."

I had many more questions, and I formed the words with my mouth, but Mom shook her head and said, "Allah will take care of us."

I obeyed. Memé was already late to elementary school, but Mom told her she'd drive her in to get the tardiness excused.

I put on a shirt that was tight around my chest. My shorts were too short. I was hungry, but there was nothing for breakfast in the house. We relied on the free school breakfast and lunch like almost everyone I knew. We were poor, but because bad food was cheap, I was a fat boy. I waited outside with my siblings while Mom gave up trying to lock the broken door behind us. Nobody spoke in the car. Mom dropped me off at the school bus stop and said, "I love you, *gordo*."

I sat on the curb and ignored the other kids. I asked Allah why this had happened to me, but he wouldn't say. I wouldn't ask again.

The school bus arrived. I had no friends on the bus. I wanted to be as strong as Dad. He told me I didn't need them, only resolute faith in Allah and myself, but I don't know how he could bear loneliness.

The kids sneered or laughed because I was different. Until I lived in Baton Rouge, I'd never known I was white.

I kept my head down and eyes up and made sure to exhale when I got within reach of those kids. Dad had taught me punches in the gut hurt less if your lungs were empty.

I sat alone in the wheel well seat. It was a thirty-minute bus ride to the middle school. I watched the streets go by, and my mind wandered.

My daydreams were happy, and things were always going to be okay. I told myself Dad hadn't escaped, and last night was just a mistake because the corrections officers had miscounted during the night rounds. I'd see him next weekend during visitation hours.

I'd learned from my maternal grandmother to tell myself these things. She learned to do it herself from her own life's tragedies. She'd lost her parents when she was barely eighteen and had her home taken away during the communist revolution in Cuba. In her elderly years, two of her children fell into drug addiction. Whenever things were tough, she told me to imagine it to be better and soon I'd see it realized. I bless her for this critical life skill, even though it was based on lies.

The bus pulled in line to drop off students. My delightful dreams receded, leaving my heart unsatisfied, like an upset stomach from too much sugar. I concocted possible courses of action now that my circumstances had changed. With Dad gone there was no reason for me to be here anymore. I was out of my element in Baton Rouge. I had grown up in Miami, and even though both Florida and Louisiana have swamps and humidity, it was like living on a different planet. I filed off the bus and tried to shrink as much as possible in the crowd.

The bayou public schools taught French instead of Spanish, and the people had accents that I'd only heard on TV. The first day of school, the homeroom teacher asked me where I had come from and why I'd moved there. I had told her it was for my dad's job.

Mom had said Louisiana was a good move because we'd be closer to Dad. We had to ride buses and trains for hours to visit him once a month when we still lived back in Florida, but in Louisiana we could see him every week, and it was only forty-five minutes away in our beat-up Honda.

I broke off from the crowd and stood in line to get my breakfast: fake scrambled eggs, white bread toast, and chocolate milk. I avoided the bacon, because I was obedient to my father that I should only eat halal food. I found the emptiest table and ate alone in the cafeteria. I tried to fill the hollow inside me with food, but afterward I still felt hungry. I wasn't used to being awake this long. I put my head down and tried to sleep.

I missed Miami and the familiar. I missed belonging somewhere. I hated the school here. I was one of the four Latino kids in the school, but I never had classes with them because I could speak English very well. The majority of the kids were Black, and they didn't like me because I looked white, and to the white kids I looked too Latino. I didn't know what I should be.

A large lunch lady shook me. "Little boy, get to class." She took my tray, and half asleep I walked to the first class before the last bell.

I didn't speak the whole day in school. I slept when I could. No one bothered me, and I didn't get fucked with for existing. I had no one to talk to about the night before. This was the kind of school where almost every kid had free or reduced-price lunch, and the teachers I had seen were only interested in following lesson plans and doling out punishments. Even if one of my teachers had asked what was wrong with me, I wouldn't have said anything anyway. A combination of fear, shame, and protecting my family ensured my silence.

In the afternoon the last bell rang, and I finished my last nap for the day. I rode the bus in the same seat I'd arrived in and passed the time counting how many streets had no sidewalks.

When I got home, the place was still messy from the raid, the door still ruined. My siblings had already returned from school and played quietly in their corners of the apartment. My mother lay on the sofa and chewed her nails down to the quick while smoking a joint so small she needed tweezers to hold it. I turned the TV on to watch afternoon cartoons.

The news was on instead.

While I sat on the floor and picked the carpet like a scab, the news anchor said Hurricane Andrew had devastated Florida and was now headed toward Louisiana.

I asked Mom what we should do, but she said nothing and just kept puffing.

The hurricane had lost its strength and was a tropical storm by the time it affected Baton Rouge on August 26.

I slept through Tropical Storm Andrew. To me it had sounded like a bad rainstorm, but we'd gotten school days off. During the night we lost power and wouldn't have it for a few days. It was hot and miserable in our little apartment.

The apartment complex had an artificial lake stocked with perch, bass, and catfish. I spent these hot and powerless days fishing with my only friend, Brandon.

Brandon was weird. He was the only Black kid in the neighborhood who wanted to hang out with me. We were the same age, and, like me, he had no father in the home. Unlike me, though, he was home-schooled. His mother worked all day and left him at home to do his studies. I don't remember ever seeing him do schoolwork. He liked to play with toys, which I found odd because most kids our age didn't anymore. When he didn't play with his action figures, we watched movies on his VCR. No matter what movie he put on, he had already memorized all the lines. When he didn't want to do that, we fished.

I knocked on his door the afternoon after the storm had passed.

"Hey, bro."

"Hey." I said nothing more because there was nothing else to do but go fishing.

"I'll grab the poles." He disappeared into his house hopping like a rabbit. His mom yelled at him unnecessarily to go outside and spend his energy somewhere else.

I never told Brandon about the raid, but in hindsight his mom probably knew and didn't care. I believe she was happy that some-one kept her son company when she had been exhausted by his eccentricities.

He returned with two poles, a cooler, and a water bottle. I took the poles and followed him. We spent that afternoon digging for worms and catching fish. We'd eat what we caught. I forgot the raid, my father, and the future.

Power returned less than a week after the storm. School hadn't started yet, and I continued being out of the house as much as possible with Brandon.

I walked into our apartment after fishing. The new dead bolt was an eyesore, bright silver against the dull brass strike plate. Mom sat on the couch, and I saw her glowing under all the makeup she wore. "Come here, *gordo*." She patted the seat beside her.

I had a habit of guessing what people wanted to hear. Before a word left her mouth, I said, "I didn't catch anything, but maybe tomorrow I'll get some catfish and you can fry it up like the last time." My mother was very proud of each catch and cooked them for dinner. "Brandon says we can try using bologna as bait, and they really like the old stuff that's gone bad. He saw some in the dumpster . . ."

"That's fine, Peté." She dismissed my words with a flick of her wrist. Mom was different today. She sat up straight and her eyes were clear, not bloodshot with dilated pupils. She was totally sober. She was dressed in jeans and a nice blouse.

"Oh." I sank lower in the couch and picked at the dirt under my fingernails.

Mom shook her head. "Fill only a backpack with clothes. We are going to Miami to visit family."

I didn't think about the things I couldn't take or about Brandon. I had grown so accustomed to having no control, I merely obeyed. Going back to Miami, where I had friends and a life before the raid, made me happy and not inclined to question her command.

She stood and fussed with her clothes until they were arranged to her preference and then walked to her room. She stopped in front of the mirror in the hallway to fix her hair. Mom had taught me beauty was in the eye of the beholder, yet at the same time she was a very vain woman.

I went to the bedroom at the back of the apartment. Memé was helping Chiní pack her clothes. Peewee played with the toys he wouldn't be taking. I emptied my school backpack of textbooks and notebooks.

I knew from the newspapers and the radio that Hurricane Andrew had devastated Miami. Mom's reason for going to Miami made no sense to me, because we had nothing to offer our family to help. My dad had been in prison since I was four, and Mom had always been on welfare. We had relied on my aunt and grandmother to help us when the government handouts had been misspent. They helped raise us when Mom couldn't handle being alone and locked herself in the bedroom during one of her bouts of depression.

We had nothing in Baton Rouge now that Dad was on the run from the feds. I had no real friends; Brandon was more of a fishing buddy than someone I was close to. I was excited because a road trip meant fast food and a change of scenery. I had no idea where my mom got the money to fund the trip, but I figured she probably skipped rent or my grandmother had spotted her the money.

Next day at the crack of dawn we loaded up our car with the bare minimum and left everything else behind. When Mom pulled out of the apartment complex, she turned off the radio. She said what I already knew.

"Okay. We're going to be with Dad."

2

I spent the time on the road daydreaming about all the fun things I'd do with my dad. I sat in the front seat by Mom. The A/C blasted, and it was cold enough for me to have to wear two shirts. I leaned my head against the window and breathed against the glass. I made smiley faces out of the fog and listed the things I saw dads on TV do with their sons: throw footballs, fish, go camping, and so on.

It didn't matter to me that I'd already learned how to do most of those things by myself or through friends. It only mattered that I did them with Dad because that's what I'd seen on TV.

The car carrying us from Baton Rouge to Miami was an old 1980s Honda sedan. The black paint had faded to gray, some of the original coat only recognizable in splotches. It fit the five of us well enough. The speakers tended to crackle at the higher pitches, but we loved listening to the radio anyway.

The closer we got to Miami, the more Spanish the lyrics got. We traveled through Reba McEntire, Whitney Houston, and ended with Gloria Estefan. Somewhere on the road between Lynyrd Skynyrd and Madonna, Mom pulled over at a gas station to fill up the car and our bellies. From the back Memé said, "Get out of my seat."

I flinched every time she reached for me. She made me feel like I had committed some crime against her, and I wasn't allowed to fight back. Mom ignored us. I got out of the car and went to the back.

This was the deal—Memé and I rotated front seat privileges

through the trip down. Mom had dictated the schedule when we'd left: whenever we needed to stop, we'd swap. It kept us from bickering and stressing her out.

I watched Memé buckle up. My childhood was an unwanted competition with her. Whether it was for a toy in a cereal box or Mom's vote for best crayon drawing, she strove to dominate. She was a year younger than I, short even for her age, chubby, and had blond locks and the same green eyes as me and our father. She was naturally gifted and had a talent for finding soft spots. I'd never hit her, but she'd hit me and leave scars. I don't remember how it started that time.

Mom had once told me we'd started fighting when Memé could barely walk and I could barely speak. She'd trash the skyscrapers I'd built with my toy blocks. I'd beg her to stop, and I'd bear-hug her and endure her two-tooth bites on my pudgy flesh until Mom came along to separate us.

Mom never attempted to correct us. She was an inattentive mother bouncing between bouts of depression and drug benders. "Peté, never hit a girl," was all she would deign to say. Memé was a force of nature to be avoided when possible and prepared for if confrontation seemed inevitable.

Mom pumped gas and watched every car that pulled up and pulled off. Chiní and Peewee sat in the backseat without complaint, and I occupied the space between them.

Chiní was six years old. She got along with me far more than Memé did. She rarely spoke. She observed everything and always had a smile. No one would suspect we were siblings.

Chiní was as brown as her brothers and sister were white. Her indigenous features are where she got her nickname. She looked like how the kids in my school expected Hispanics to appear. Our differences never bothered me, and no one dug too deep to find out why Chiní looked different from all my mother's other children.

Peewee was just shy of three. He too smiled at everyone. Until I had children of my own, his birth was the happiest day of my life. When Mom was pregnant with him, I was old enough to have a rudimentary understanding of what was happening in our family: a new life was arriving. I was doubly excited because it was a boy, and I had always wanted a brother to play with. I'd looked forward to sharing my toys with Peewee, teaching him how to ride a bike, throw a football, and all the mandatory foolishness of boyhood.

On the day of Peewee's birth, Mom went to the hospital like everyone I knew had. After we received news of his birth, we'd been told Peewee had been born sick. Mom had used crack during her pregnancy. The doctors kept him in the NICU at Jackson Memorial Hospital for three months, and I don't know how Mom avoided getting us all taken away from her and becoming wards of the state.

Mom finished filling up the car and passed food around before turning the key in the ignition. She pulled out of the gas station and continued to move toward what had been, to me, home.

We stopped at another motel before it got dark and ate fast food again. Dad preferred we ate at Burger King. He said they didn't use animal lard for all their cooking and thus was halal. That night, Mom fed us McDonald's because it was closer. We left the motel the next day before the sun was up.

As we approached Miami, I stopped trading spots with Memé. I was content to be in the back and watch the cars go by, getting used as a pillow by Chiní and Peewee. Memé had problems tolerating my existence, but they accepted me.

We crossed into Miami–Dade County, and Mom turned the music off. The destruction from Hurricane Andrew had erased the landscape I'd remembered from a few months earlier. Many windows were still boarded up or missing altogether. Shops were closed. People wandered to lines for food and water. The traffic lights that hadn't been blown away didn't work. Florida National Guard troops drove through the streets in Hummers outfitted with loudspeakers. They held the same kind of rifles as the men who had broken into our home in Baton Rouge. Cop cars were parked everywhere. Mom said there would be no stops for gasoline, food, or bathroom breaks. She followed the signs to Miami Beach and drove straight to my maternal grandparents' home.

This was before Miami Beach had become the party town known as South Beach. Most of the people who lived there at that time were elderly, and there were more synagogues than bars. Quiet Hasidic Jews strolled on the sidewalks, and the only street music came from the Hare Krishnas chanting and clashing their finger cymbals.

There were no dedicated parking spots for the apartment building. Mom found one just off Washington Avenue. We laughed as Mom tried to parallel park. She said *fuck* every time she had to reverse or go forward, which made us laugh even more. I knew she was in a good mood because she didn't bark at us to shut up. Finally satisfied with the parking job, she shut down the car and we walked to the entrance.

Normally the door to the building required either a key or using a callbox, but management had left the doors wide open. There still was no electricity, and the slight breeze from outside helped cool the foyer.

The building was named Blackstone. It wasn't painted black but a kind of color that reminded me of peach yogurt. It was fourteen stories tall and used to be one of the tallest buildings in Miami Beach. In the 1930s it had been a luxury hotel. Inside the foyer there was still evidence of the Gilded Age in the banister and columns. Gaudy decorations were lacquered onto the baseboards and light fixtures. It could've been a million-dollar condo, but instead it was Section 8 housing.

Old Cuban men and women lounged in *batas* and unbuttoned guayabera shirts. They all wore expressions of exhausted solitude. A haze of boredom clouded their eyes. The air smelled of urine and stale sweat. Their misery wasn't caused by the hurricane's destruction or inconveniences. The tenants here had always looked this way when I had visited, and I imagined my grandparents looked this way when we weren't around.

Mom held Peewee and Chiní's hands. We looked at no one. Memé was admiring the echoes of the cavernous lobby, but my mom silenced her with a hush. She rushed us through, and we made our way to the elevators that still functioned through a backup generator.

We argued among ourselves for the privilege of pushing the button to my grandparents' floor. "It's my turn," Memé asserted. I didn't bother arguing and reached for the button, but she seized my arm with her sharp nails and broke a scab from a previous tussle we'd had in the car.

I cried out, "You fat bitch!"

"Hey, stop it," Mom said.

Memé let go. I cradled my arm and watched the blood ooze from the old wound. Memé stared at me with a smile.

Mom asked if Chiní wanted to push the button, but she kept her head down. Peewee didn't wait to be asked and reached out to press number eleven. The door closed and the elevator lurched into motion. We ascended in silence and listened to the invisible machinery around us.

My grandparents' apartment was the first door by the elevator. My grandmother, Alle, opened the door after one knock. We rushed in and hugged her.

Alle had always insisted we speak only Spanish to her, and we obliged. She cried, "My little ones!" My grandfather, Abo, came up from behind and joined in the hugging.

They let us inside their two-bedroom, one-bathroom apartment. It was still decorated with old furniture and relics of their better days in Cuba. Pictures hung on the walls from a time when Abo had owned a prosperous restaurant and the family was whole. These images were from long before communism, drugs, and business failures had condemned him to the poverty of an early retirement. They hugged us some more and kissed us. Mom gave them cordial hugs, the kind that I recognized as polite among Hispanics who were at least associates.

Abo had cooked a lunch of beans and rice for us, probably with a portable gas stove. They smiled and watched us as we ate silently.

After the meal we sat around the living room. Memé and Chiní played with strings of yarn, and Peewee sat silently watching the girls make puzzling patterns between their hands. I took my usual perch in a chair by the window looking out to the sea. It was my favorite spot to daydream.

Alle had opened the window, and the ocean breeze cooled the sweat off my skin. I watched the waves and the people. My stomach and heart were full. I didn't know why we had come here to see my grandparents, and I didn't much care about details.

The adults went to the small kitchen and talked in low voices.

Mom needed to tell Alle the whole truth. She did so because my dad was going to need help evading the feds, and Mom knew that Alle and Abo were first and foremost loyal to the family. They never said no to her.

Later that night we slept on their living room floor, all five of us in a heap, much like that night in Baton Rouge. Sleep came quick. We were exhausted from traveling and eager to see Dad.

We set out from Miami Beach after we ate breakfast—the last of their eggs and butter on Cuban bread. Alle and Abo walked us down to the car and gave us hugs and Hershey's chocolate bars for the road. The chocolate felt soft from the heat.

From the curb Alle said to Mom, "Be careful, Lele." The car started and Mom pulled away.

Memé sat in the front seat and found a radio station playing Madonna. "Where are we going now?"

Mom breathed deep and blew a kiss to Memé. "We're going to Kendall."

I sighed. "Is Dad there?"

Mom winked. "After Dad arrived at Miami in the middle of the hurricane, he hid with Marta."

Mom explained to me years later that Marta adored my father. She felt grateful for my father bringing her grandsons into the world—my two older half brothers Adrian and JP. Dad took advantage of this gratitude and used his charm to get favors from her from time to time. She overlooked the abandonment, the abuse, and neglect of his sons and her daughter. Anything of hers was Dad's if he but asked.

"Why is he there?" I recognized Marta's name and knew she was my two older half brothers' grandmother. It seemed strange to me that an elderly woman would help a man who had divorced her daughter. Divorce seemed a final cut with families, at least it was on TV and with the parents of the kids I knew. Mom told a story to pass the time on our drive out of Miami Beach.

My mother lit a cigarette and rolled down the windows. "Dad met his first wife, Gini, when he was fifteen. Her mother, Marta, found him charming. I mean, *loved* him."

Memé turned the radio down, and the little ones leaned forward to listen.

Mom turned off the A/C and kept looking down at the gas gauge. She continued. "Gini's father hated Dad's guts, but he wanted to make his daughter happy. Dad got Gini pregnant at sixteen. They married before Adrian was born. A few years later Dad had a second son, you know, JP."

Mom stopped at an intersection and waited for the cop to wave traffic through. She said nothing more until Memé spoke. "What happened?"

Mom flicked her ashes out the window. "Well, after a while Gini left him, and the boys went with Marta for a while in Puerto Rico."

The cop waved us through, and Mom drove slowly past him. "Marta's husband died, and she moved back here with the boys. Then they lived with us for a while, when you were a little baby, Memé, and, Peté, you were two."

"And me?" Peewee asked.

She blew him a kiss from the rearview mirror. "No, my beautiful Peewee and Chiní weren't ready yet."

Peewee smiled and Chiní asked how long ago.

Mom answered her and abruptly lowered her voice, the way Dad did when he would say he was being deadly serious. "Listen, do not bring up Adrian around Marta. She will have a nervous breakdown if you bring it up."

I remembered being told the story years before. Dad was high and asleep. Adrian, a headstrong thirteen-year-old boy, took his dirt bike out in the rain. He couldn't see where he was going and hit a wall, dying instantly. Dad had to run from the cops when they came to inform him of his firstborn son's death.

Mom flicked the cigarette out the window when we hit the I-95 and said, "I think Marta really adores Dad because he's the only connection left to her beloved Adrian."

After the tale, we continued in silence and Memé turned the radio back on. My mother drove the speed limit to avoid getting pulled over and blowing the whole escape.

I spent the time on the road watching the storm wreckage left behind. I swiveled my head window to window and wondered how hard the winds had to have been to be able to knock down ancient banyan trees that were wider than the car. The destruction of so many homes and businesses made Miami seem like the war zones on TV.

Finally, we arrived at Marta's condo. The complex had been largely spared from the hurricane and still had electricity. It was in a community of well-off retired Cubans, the opposite of my grandmother's government-funded apartment building.

Marta possessed an inheritance from her long-dead husband, the man who had known my dad was no good for his girl. We pulled in and parked in the guest spot for her place. Mom spent a long time fixing herself up with the rearview mirror. We were all impatient, anxious to see Dad.

We walked what seemed like a block to the doorway, and Mom rang the bell. Marta opened the door, though I expected Dad to be the one to do it. She smiled at us and embraced us children in one hug, showering us with affection as if she were in fact our blood grandmother. She and Mom kissed and embraced more deeply than Mom had with Alle. We were family, but mostly in Marta's head.

"Come in, come in! Wow, how beautiful you all are!" Marta kissed each of us on both cheeks. Her kindness wasn't fake. I had already learned how to tell from my mom's past party-girl friends. When people gave me a compliment, it often turned into a means to get something from me, but with Marta I felt she truly loved us. I believed this woman and Alle were cut from the same cloth.

Marta closed the door behind us and called Dad. "Evaristo, it's your beautiful family."

Dad emerged barefoot from one of the back rooms of the apartment. He wore light khaki pants and a pastel blue polo shirt. His dark hair was slicked back, and his trimmed goatee framed his smile. On his wrist was a silver Rolex watch. The same eyes as mine seemed to glow blue green. After seeing him wear prison uniforms for so long, the vibrant colors made him appear divine. As if he had been resurrected.

Dad said, "As-salamu-aliakum," and we were home.

We rushed at him. He choked out the words, "Careful with my knee." We hugged and kissed and cried. If I could freeze that moment, I'd hang it on a wall and believe that I was a happy child from a happy family.

3

We spent the night at Marta's. I slept in the living room on a futon with my siblings. Mom and Dad had the spare room to themselves. I remembered watching the TV with the volume turned up when they were alone in there.

After that night, Mom became a different woman. Next morning, she walked out of the room with a glow I hadn't seen on her before. This was the first time I had seen her happy, and I could tell by the size of her pupils it wasn't drugs. She wasn't short tempered with us anymore. She hugged us, and I couldn't remember her hugging me before without me seeking the affection first. I didn't recognize it at the time, but Dad was the ultimate high for her.

Marta for the most part kept to herself. She only emerged from her bedroom to go out with her friends in the afternoon or to cook dinner for us. My siblings and I were content for a few days. Eventually we grew bored. One late morning we screamed at each other, and Memé put her nails into my forearm. She tore open old wounds that hadn't had the chance to heal. Chiní and Peewee stayed quiet on the couch and pretended like nothing had happened.

Dad yelled from his room and his door flew open. The house flooded with the smell of weed. "Who died?" He held a lit roach clamped in a pair of pliers.

"He started it," Memé said. She sneered at me and looked like she had crushed a bug.

"No, that's a lie." I gave her the middle finger, the tip covered in blood and scabs.

Mom followed behind Dad. She wore one of Marta's robes. "Guys, we can't be yelling. The neighbors will call the cops."

Mom's ultimate parenting tool: she told us that if one of us got too far out of line, Dad would go back to prison. Worse, she had said, she too would go to prison. We'd become wards of the state and probably be sexually molested by foster parents. It was a powerful tool.

Mom placed her hand on Dad's shoulder, but he turned to her and shook his head. He always dug deeper. "No, what is happening?" He changed his posture, and he grew wider and louder. "Why are you hurting each other? You're brother and sister."

Memé and I didn't answer. We never lied about our fights, and we had no capacity to understand our dysfunction.

Dad got a paper towel roll from the kitchen and threw it at me. "Clean yourself up." He sat between us on the couch and lit his roach again. "I had six brothers and sisters." He took a deep hit and held it in long enough for me to think he wasn't ever going to exhale. He choked and then released rings of smoke into the air. "Do either of you know what I regret most?"

These were my answers—prison, drug addiction, or being an absent father—but I didn't say any of that. My answers weren't what he wanted to hear. Always, whether in a prison visit, a letter, or a collect call, his questions to me were rhetorical. Memé didn't answer either.

"I never got close to my siblings." Dad paused and drilled his eyes into each of us. Mom sat next to the two little ones after both had moved to the carpeted floor, away from the scene on the couch. She smiled at us and had a contented look, the kind she put on when watching her favorite TV show.

Dad continued, "Today, if I ran into my brother walking in the street, he wouldn't even look at me." He took another hit and let it go quickly. "Like if I was some dead dog on the side of the road."

He slapped his knee with the hand holding the roach, and it flew off into the carpet. He picked it up, wiped the ashes off the carpet with his fingers, and placed it back in the pliers. "My own sisters wouldn't piss on me if I was on fire."

I'd heard he'd been kicked out of his family at sixteen after his father had died, but he never said why he'd been abandoned. All I knew at the time was that his parents were on the older side when he, the seventh child, came into the world. His siblings were much older than he was, and he was practically raised by the youngest teenaged sister.

When he saw no reaction from us, he asked Memé, "Why did you do that to your brother?" He lifted the paper towel off my arms, ripping off the dried blood.

"He called me a fat bitch." Memé pointed at me like a victim on the stand in a crime procedural TV show I'd seen called *Law and Order*.

Dad didn't bother to cross-examine the witness like the slick lawyers on the show. I remembered he'd said everyone in his family had practiced law. Dad faced me. "Why would you say that to your sister?"

"She called me Peteta." It was her favorite insult. It was my nickname feminized and fused with the Spanish word for tits. Because I had tits, it made sense. I'd already been taught by the kids at playground parking lots and public school classrooms: no boy ever wants to have any trait remotely feminine.

Dad turned to Memé. Before he could speak, she said, "I wanted to watch music videos on TV."

We now started talking past and over each other, competing for Dad's attention. He boomed, "Enough!" Memé and I were startled into silence. It was like he had gone Mach 2 and laid us out. It blasted through the bickering and bullshit.

Dad pointed to the carpet of the living room. "Peté, drop and give me ten."

His eyebrows raised when I didn't jump to his order. No man had ever spoken to me in that manner before. Even when he sat me down at prison visits to lecture me, he'd adopted a persuasive and reasonable tone. Now that he walked free, his voice mimicked the way corrections officers told inmates visiting hours had ended or the military drill instructors I'd caught glimpses of on TV barked at enlistees.

"I didn't do anything!"

Dad's lips curled into a smile. "I'm not making you push because you treated your sister like some whore in the street. Still, you don't talk to your sister that way." He pointed to the carpeted floor again.

"But why?" I barely said the words and went down on all fours. I raised my head and saw Memé's triumphant smile. Of course. She had won him over and I was at her mercy. Again.

He said, "If you're so insecure about your tits, you'll work on getting rid of them. I'll make sure." Dad took another hit. "Don't cry. Real men don't cry." He turned to Memé, and she gave him the sweetest look. "What the fuck are you looking at?" She froze and her face reminded me of a discarded doll staring at nothing. "You are a piece of shit. You hurt your brother because you know he won't hit back. He loves you that much and you do this to him."

Memé couldn't get more than a few words out.

Dad ignored her. She hated being ignored. He stood, walked over to the kitchen, and discarded the roach in the sink. "No music videos. Music is un-Islamic." This was one of his hypocrisies. I knew he loved music, but at that moment it was as final as if a fatwa had been issued from Mecca itself.

I tried and failed to do one push-up. Memé laughed.

Dad whistled. "Lean up against the wall." I did so, and he turned to Memé: "Next time you hurt your brother like that I will cut your nails off completely. Then you'll be like one of those stray cats no one gives a fuck about and abandons. You understand?"

No one had ever spoken to her like that before either. Dad had always been gentle with his words to her. Strangers adored her curly blond hair, dimpled smile, and blue eyes. They called her Shirley Temple sometimes. Now she had no rebuttal or witty retort, and Dad ignored the baby doll looks she relied on to soften hard hearts.

The rest of the family had watched this and said nothing. Mom smiled. I finished my ten wall push-ups, and Dad made Memé finish cleaning the blood off my arm.

No one spoke further about this, and I played with Peewee while Dad cooked. Memé and Chiní had their dolls, and Mom sat smoking a cigarette, watching her man be a father to his children.

Next morning Dad shook me awake. I smelled the coffee on his breath before I saw him. "Wake up, son. Get up."

Only the oven lamp was on in the condo. He sat on the futon and sipped from a white mug that was stained yellow along the rim. In that light, the contours of my father's face had a harshness, like he was a natural creature of the shadow. My siblings were still asleep.

"What happened?" I sat straight up. It had only been a few weeks since the raid, and waking up before dawn still rattled my nerves.

Dad spoke with force that felt like a slap and yet was not loud. "Is there something wrong with your hearing?" He wore gray sweatpants and an undershirt so white it glowed brighter than the oven light. "Wake up, son. Get up."

"What did I do wrong?"

Dad slowly rose from the futon, giving his bad knee time to adjust from sitting. "You're slow. When I say to do something, I demand you do it immediately. Understand?"

I didn't know how to answer, so I said, "I'm sorry."

"I know you're a sorry boy." Dad limped toward the kitchen and I got up and followed.

The floor went from thick warm carpet to marble tile. Dad leaned against the sink and said, "Take off your shirt."

"Why?"

Dad knocked back the remainder of his coffee and placed the mug in the sink quietly. I couldn't meet his eyes anymore. They were deep in his face and bright like the eyes of stray cats in the night. I took off my T-shirt and stood in the kitchen wearing only my dirty briefs. I covered what I could of my bulk with my arms.

Dad took my measure. I knew what he saw: a fleshy boy with tits and thick thighs that barely fit in boys' size underwear. His thin eyebrows met, and it reminded me of the looks I got from everyone after Mom forced me to take my T-shirt off when I was at the pool or beach. He didn't like what he saw, and I was afraid of his disappointment.

Mom had told me once that my father had an honor code to never hit his women or children, but she had said he had other ways of disciplining.

I kept my head down, and our breaths conversed like how I think sons and their disappointed fathers do: shallow breaths apologized, deep and slow breaths judged.

Dad finally broke the silence. "Drop and give me ten."

"Again?"

He pointed to the tile. The muscles on his forearm bulged, like an exclamation point. "Get on your face. Do ten push-ups. They taught you this in school, right?"

The tile felt cold against my chest, and it smelled a little like bleach. I put my arms out to the side like a lizard and tried to push away. It felt like someone had glued me to the floor.

I heard Dad's head shaking. "Do it like a girl."

I obeyed and barely did one push-up from my knees. I flopped down; my bulk slapped the tiles like a chunk of slime from a Nickelodeon game show. I looked up to him after I caught my breath. "I'm sorry."

"Don't be sorry. Be strong." From down on the floor, Dad seemed so much larger and powerful than me. He gestured with his palm as if he were raising the dead. "Lean against the wall again and do ten."

On all fours like an animal, I crawled and used the countertop to help me up. I did ten push-ups against the wall, but I was out of breath by the last one. My heart pounded so hard I thought it would break out of my ribcage.

I turned to Dad and leaned back.

He said, "Every morning, before you feed yourself or turn on the TV you will do push-ups. If you can walk, do so for thirty minutes. Do you understand?"

After the first sound left my lips, I stopped talking. I'd already learned to drop the reflex to ask what I had done to deserve punishment. I nodded and Dad opened the fridge and pulled out a large glass mixing bowl. It looked like it was full of puke.

"This is your breakfast. Oatmeal."

"I want Fruit Loops."

Dad snapped his head up at me. "You eat what I give you and nothing else."

I was smart enough not to ask for sugar or syrup with my oatmeal. "Can I put my T-shirt back on?"

"Yeah." Dad transferred the oatmeal to a small bowl and used the microwave to heat it up. We watched the timer count down in silence. I was fascinated by the appliance. It invisibly cooked and sounded cool to me with the humming and beeping. It reminded me of the replicators and food processors I'd seen on *Star Trek*.

Technology had always been an affinity of mine. All my toys and TV shows were of brave heroes overcoming obstacles through the clever use of gadgets and computers: *Star Trek*, *Batman*, *G.I. Joe*, and *Transformers* all used tech and courage to get out of sticky situations.

The memory of Dad's harshness faded with my curiosity. "Dad, how do microwaves work?"

He turned to me. "It uses electromagnetic radiation, microwave band, to heat the water molecules in food." I had heard the terms he used on TV, so I could follow along with him though not completely understand.

Unlike my mother and everyone else in my family, Dad had a broad encyclopedic knowledge of things. Mom had told me years earlier that he had dropped out of school before he was fourteen. It was his time in prison that had attracted him to erudition. He read widely on many topics, and if he got bored with something he would move on to a completely different topic. I know this now to mean he was a polymath and naturally gifted. If he didn't know something, he'd find a book in a library or an encyclopedia article and would soon find out.

The beep interrupted my next question of how the microwave produced the radiation. Dad sat me down at the breakfast table with my plain oatmeal. "Eat all of it."

It was still dark and the whole house was still asleep. Dad went back to the room he shared with Mom, and he returned with a rolled-up prayer rug. He opened the sliding glass door to the backyard. It was the only private place he could do his prayers in the morning. He adjusted the rug so that he would face in the direction of Mecca, somewhere far to the east and away from this world. He closed the door behind him so he wouldn't wake anyone, though he prayed quietly so the neighbors wouldn't be suspicious of someone speaking Arabic in a Cuban neighborhood.

I watched him go down onto his knees slowly. He looked like I did when I tried to get up after push-ups. His back was to me, but I could imagine the pained expression on his face.

Dad held his hands up and quietly recited the call to prayers.

The day after our fight and my push-ups, Memé brought up birthday party planning with Dad. Chiní's birthday and Memé's were only a few days away. They were born two years and a day apart, but they never fought over the attention.

I am the only child of the summer. My father had two sons before me, Adrian and JP. Mom had four kids: me, Memé, and Peewee from Dad, and Chiní. All my siblings were born in autumn, all born in the month of September, except for Adrian in October. I realize now that to my father they were children of summer because he was born and raised in the Southern Hemisphere. Perhaps to him I was his only child of winter.

"Birthdays are un-Islamic." Dad sat on the couch with the girls, while Peewee and I played on the floor. Mom sat on the counter drinking coffee.

"But we always had parties." Memé leaned against Dad and played with his hair.

Dad smiled. "To celebrate what? How much your mother suffered to bring you into the world?"

Memé wouldn't let it go. "But she was happy to celebrate."

Dad turned his body toward Memé, but he spoke to all of us. "Listen. All this birthday celebration anxiety is a crock of shit. Every day Allah put you on his earth is a celebration. This fixation on parties and toys is just a ploy to make your parents waste money on frivolity. And it's haram."

Memé glanced at Mom. Dad hummed and raised an eyebrow. Mom cleared her throat. "Eva, it's not that big of a deal. The kids like it."

Dad pointed at Mom. "You should throw *this woman* a party for delivering you."

I had just enjoyed my eleventh birthday party a few months earlier. Only my grandparents were there, but they'd treated me to a whole tub of flan from a bakery in Calle Ocho and a video game rental.

"Let me be perfectly clear to you," Dad said as he gently set Memé away from him. "While I am captain of this ship, we will not be practicing this fake celebration of life."

The walls of the living room seemed smaller now.

"What are we going to do on our birthdays then?" I knew as soon as I said it—I shouldn't have spoken.

"We're going to survive." Dad's volume blew away any thought of compromise.

No one had set harsh rules or severely changed my celebrations before. It made me want to cry, but he'd already told me real men don't cry.

He said, "Do any of you think I love you less because I won't do this? Don't I buy you shit whenever you need it? Let me tell you all: I am doing this precisely because I love you more." Dad stood up; he moved slowly not only because of his bad knees but to intimidate us. "If I didn't love you, I'd just buy you shit you don't need and call it a day. I'm trying to make your soul strong." He walked and limped to the bedroom. Mom followed him.

We sat around the rest of the day defeated, but we hardened our hearts. We never celebrated a birthday with our father.

Dad and I were always the first to rise. I told no one about the morning exercises while we were at Marta's condo. My silence hid the weaknesses and disappointment I felt from my father's eyes. In retrospect it wasn't necessary.

The lack of physical fitness and craving for my father's approval proved impossible to conceal from Memé. She never missed an opportunity to comment on my flabbiness, my weakness. She was chubby as well, but somehow this didn't interfere with her fitness. She had always overpowered me despite age and gender. Sometimes she got Chiní and Peewee to tease me too, and those attacks were always the worst to endure. I had dealt with these by becoming a scarce target. In other words, I ran away often or wasn't around much. But now, in the small condo and on the run from the law thanks to Dad's escape, I was forced to confront my sister and what a fat piece of shit I was. We fought over food, for TV time, for attention. Sometimes we fought because we were bored.

Dad had trouble keeping the peace. He'd intervene, drop another anecdote about fighting with his brothers, and repeat himself. It made no difference, and we screamed at each other just the same after he'd leave us alone.

Marta spent the days away visiting her friends. She eventually told us the loudness coming from her home attracted the attention of her friends. They asked uncomfortable questions. She lied and told them it was one of her cousin's grandchildren. Within a week she sat Dad down and told him the kids were going to get us all burned. Even if we were the most perfectly behaved children, Dad knew we could not stay in her small home forever. He grew restless.

Dad spent the days flipping through the pages of a little black address book. Within it lay the names, numbers, and addresses of all the contacts he had in the drug trafficking profession. Mom had held on to it and kept it safe during his years of confinement in federal prison. After our morning workouts and prayers, his attention focused solely on the black book. He never called people from the condo, instead preferring to risk a walk to the nearest pay phone.

Before leaving for the first time to walk to the pay phone, Dad stopped at the door and pointed at me. "I shall return."

I said, "Okay."

"Do you know who said that?"

"You did."

He barked a laugh. "No. General Douglas MacArthur. He said that to his troops, the ones he left behind on the battlefield. He said, 'I shall return.' And you know what?"

"What?"

"He did, at the head of an army. Remember that." He jiggled the keys to the door and dropped his voice to a low bass. "I shall return."

Mom looked like she would pull her hair out for the next thirty to forty minutes while he was away, but he did return. He came back without an army and rather annoyed and irritated. Only after he and Mom had disappeared into the bedroom would his mood improve.

A few days after Marta's warning, Dad returned from making one of his calls. This time he came through the door with a satisfied smile and sauntered in like a stray cat after catching a bird. He sat next to me on the couch.

Chiní, Peewee, and I had been watching afternoon cartoons on cable, an unspeakably wonderful luxury I had never had before. The shows were better than the ones on broadcast TV. Reruns of *Star Trek* played at night. Even the commercials were more entertaining.

"Son, we're going to run errands." He pointed to my shoes by the door, which was his way of ordering me to get moving.

Mom overheard this from the room, where she spent the time smoking weed to calm her nerves while Dad was out. She walked out with Memé behind her. "Where are you taking him?"

Dad held her gaze for a long time without speaking. He had the same smile he wore walking in.

"I want to come too," Memé piped in.

He didn't break eye contact from Mom. "No," he said.

"Be careful," Mom finally said, and she returned to the room with Memé. Dad pointed again to the shoes and followed Mom and Memé back to the room.

I went outside after putting my shoes on and saw the car doors were unlocked. In the front seat I toyed with the cigarette lighter and waited. I rolled down the window and laughter came in.

Kids from the neighborhood were playing outside. The way they laughed was like Hurricane Andrew had never happened, except to other people somewhere else far away. Judging from their size they were about the same age as me. They played football with a Nerf ball that whistled as it moved through the air. Their clothes and shoes were clean. They had nice haircuts. I still had stubble on my scalp from my mom's buzz cut, and my clothes were a year and a size off. When I saw other kids, I wondered how they lived and if they were happier than me. I didn't envy or hate them because of the material wealth they so obviously had. I wanted to know why I couldn't have those things too, along with a family that provided it.

Dad opened the driver's side door and avoided placing too much weight on his knee while getting in. The car bounced as he adjusted the seat. He peered at the neighborhood kids and gave a dismissive smile. Dad turned the key in the ignition. "Ready, soldier?"

Since starting our morning physical training schedule, he'd taken to using military terms with me. I thought it was cool and was happy to have that role in the family. "Where are we going?"

Dad put on his Ray-Bans. "I already told you." He backed out of the parking space without using the rearview mirror.

"I meant, what are we going to do? The errands." The car backed up so fast, my stomach felt like it was being tossed out of my body, like I was on a roller coaster.

"That's the right question." Dad stopped reversing and drove forward through the complex. He turned on the radio and Creedence Clearwater Revival played on an oldies station. He banged the steering wheel to the rhythm.

I waited for the answer as we drove past the kids in the condo complex. They watched me as I watched them while we pulled out of the parking lot. Their smiles seemed content, but at the same time their eyes were small and mean, as if they knew I didn't belong there.

The exit gates opened, and Dad drove on. "I need to go out and find a way to make money." He raised the volume slightly and sang along to the CCR lyrics—"It ain't me. It ain't me. I ain't no senator's son."

I thought about what it meant to be making money. I knew money was essential to life, like food and water, but I didn't understand it. I did know how my father made money, though I had never had the courage before to ask why. "Dad, why do you sell drugs for money?"

FUGITIVE SON

Dad lowered the volume, and the engine and air-conditioner fan replaced the music. Along sidewalks and atop utility poles, workers repaired damage from the hurricane. An angry horn accompanied by a venomous stream of curses in Spanish got Dad's attention, and he looked quickly at the driver behind, then at me. "I don't sell drugs. That's street dealers. I traffic them. I supply dealers." His posture was straight, and his chest puffed out like a proud bull fighter.

"I know. I just mean . . ."

He cut me off. "No, you don't." He chuckled and leaned in a little toward me. "You don't know."

"Isn't it haram to do drugs?" I used the term for items and behavior forbidden in Islamic law to impress him and show that I did read the religious material he had assigned me over the years.

"It's pronounced ha-RAM. Say it." I obeyed. "Good. Yes, it is haram." He reached for the radio knob but stopped himself before turning up the volume.

We turned onto the ramp to I-95 South. "Then why do you do it?" I watched his fingers tap to a rhythm only he heard.

Dad smiled, and he explained with his hands as if trying to shape something in the air. "Nobody is perfect, son, except for the Prophet Mohammad, Sal-Allahu-Alayhi was Salaam. We will all be measured by Allah on the day of judgment." He once told me he kept his nails short because it's better for fighting and avoiding sickness from eating with your hands.

"Still, it's a sin to do what you do, right?"

He patted my thigh and nodded. "Yes. You are wise, you know that?"

His praise was a hit, a high. I rode on and let the conversation flow. "Then why do you do it?"

"Allah, Subhan Allah, has a plan for all of us. We can't comprehend it. We all have a role in it."

His logic upset my world's order. Growing up, everything was presented to me as good or evil. No one had ever talked to me in these terms. "So, your role is a criminal?"

"Yes." He pointed up. "Think about it—without me, who would the cops go after?"

I laughed. "I guess there would be no cops."

"Exactly. I give them purpose. A reason to wake up in the morning." He gripped the steering wheel with both hands and squeezed.

"So, if there were no criminals there'd be no cops?"

Dad scoffed. "And now you realize the game we are trapped in. The powers that be will never allow that. Someone will always be the criminal."

"You mean the government wants there to be criminals?"

His eyes grew wide. "Absolutely. They do it to maintain power. They keep people in fear."

My little mind was blown away, of course. Dad was more knowledgeable and wiser than I could conceive, certainly more than my teachers in elementary school. The idea that life wasn't so black and white, that a human being's occupation wasn't what made him evil, wasn't taught in school. I gawked at this philosopher criminal and felt something in my chest I would call pride in my father. As I grew older and a little wiser in the ways of human beliefs, I realized he was a junkie for conspiracy theories. To him any story that could fit his narrative must be true. Still, he had a point.

Dad turned the radio volume back up. The CCR song had ended during our talk, and he tuned in another station. Duran Duran was playing, and my father sang along with the song. Before it finished, he tuned in another station. He had a habit of not allowing songs to finish.

While he sang and switched stations and banged on the steering wheel, I watched my surroundings but saw nothing. Our talk disturbed me, and my mind felt strapped into a roller coaster like when we sped out of the parking spot at Marta's. I wouldn't focus until I noticed Dad had stopped the music. We were on a one-lane road in the more rural parts of Miami, past Tamiami Trail and close to the Everglades. There were no construction barriers or police to manage the traffic at the dysfunctional stoplights.

The homes were large, with larger yards, and most were gated and surrounded with walls instead of fences. They weren't fancy like the mansions I'd seen around Miami Beach or on TV shows like *Magnum P.I.* The closest comparison I had was from watching *Cops*: on that show they called these places compounds.

We pulled in to one of these compounds through an open gate. This place had no walls and seemed familiar to me. Dad turned off the car. "Okay, we're only going to be here for a minute and then we're moving on."

"Who lives here?"

Dad let out a sigh that made him seem smaller. "An old friend. You don't remember Mohammad?"

I remembered. Mohammad was in prison with Dad during one of his incarcerations before I was born. Mom had visited him here once eight years ago, and Dad had still been behind bars. I was young, and she had brought us kids along to play with his children. I never found out what the purpose of her business then had been. Mohammad's children were boring, but he had ostriches roaming in an enclosure in his backyard and a tiger in a cage. The only other detail I remembered was that Mohammad's brother had just gone to join the mujahidin in Afghanistan to fight the Soviets.

Bright tropical plants lined the walkway to Mohammad's door. I spotted iguanas hanging out in the sun on decorative rocks. They didn't scare me much, and I liked that they ate bugs. The door opened, and a middle-aged Arab man embraced my father. "As-salamu-aliakum, Frank." He called my father by his anglicized middle name of Francisco. His dark hair and well-groomed beard were flecked with gray, though he seemed no older than my father.

Dad patted his back hard, the way he hugged those he loved. "As-salamu-aliakum, Mohammad." They released each other, and my father put his arm around my shoulder. "This is my son, Peté."

I made my bulk as small as possible under my fat. Mohammad smiled, and it felt genuine to me. He reached out his hand and greeted me like my father did. I shook his hand and mumbled back the appropriate reply in Arabic.

Mohammad handed my father a large brown paper shopping bag. They embraced one more time, but with less back slapping. Dad turned and we went back to the car. I sat in the car while Dad placed the paper bag in the trunk.

I knew on some level that Dad didn't want me to know what was in the paper bag. If he had wanted me to know, he'd tell me, so I didn't ask.

Dad got in the car and turned the key. "What was that?" he asked.

"What was what?"

He reversed the car out of Mohammad's driveway. "Don't make some face like there's a fucking camera pointed at you."

"What did I do?"

Dad accelerated so fast my body was pushed against the seat. "Don't be a bitch. Don't be shy like that to another man."

"I'm sorry."

"Don't be sorry. Be a fucking man. Only bitches and faggots act like that in front of another man. Be confident. You say 'As-salamu-aliakum' to another Muslim, say it like you mean it. Not like some faggot."

I kept my face away from him and pretended to look out the window.

Dad slapped his chest. "Look at me."

I did so.

His eyes were cold, and when he spoke, I noticed the coffee and nicotine stains on his crooked bottom teeth. "If you don't, no one will take you serious and they'll think you're weak. Don't be weak. I'm telling you this because I love you."

"I love you too, Dad."

Dad seemed satisfied with this answer and tuned the radio to a jazz station. We listened to an old jazz performance that I thought I'd heard in old episode of a *Tom and Jerry* cartoon.

It was getting late. I was hungry, but I didn't want the embarrassment of a fat kid asking for food. We drove in silence listening to music, changing the radio station every other song. I didn't recognize the street names Dad drove on anymore. The homes were less damaged, and the stores were all open. Streetlights here worked, and I saw neither reconstruction crews nor soldiers. I thought we had gone all the way to Fort Lauderdale, but the billboard advertisements were still in Spanish. Just as the sun had turned everything pink, Dad pulled into a gated community of condos.

The community was enclosed by walls taller than any man and had a creamy color. Neatly trimmed hedges hugged the false stucco surface of the walls, and a green lawn ran all the way to the road. It looked like no hurricane had come close to this area.

The gatehouse matched the wall and landscaping. By contrast, the guard was an old, sloppy-looking Cuban man. He stumbled out of the sliding glass door with a clipboard. Dad told him a number that I thought could only be the next errand. The guard wrote down the number, and he lifted the gate arm. He had sat down before we drove on.

There were no children playing. There were no minivans in the parking spots I saw and no bicycles left unattended on the sidewalks. Everything here was adult, and I felt like I was trespassing in a wealthy neighbor's backyard.

Dad parked in a designated guest parking space and shut the engine off. He let out a sigh again like he had at Mohammad's. "All right, Peté. I know you're a good boy, so I don't got to tell you to behave. Just be cool. All right?"

I nodded. "Who are we seeing? Another friend?"

Dad pressed his lips into a line. "No, this guy is a business associate. Understand?" He went to the trunk to get the bag from Mohammad.

We walked to a turquoise door. The knocker on it was shaped like a turtle's shell. Dad used the doorbell button next to it instead and smiled at the peephole. Before he rang a second time a dead-bolt clicked, and a chain jingled.

A pale man with eyes the color of ice opened the door. He was skinny and dressed like the lawyers I saw on cop shows, but I didn't think he was an attorney; he had scars on his knuckles. He reminded me of a wolf I once saw in a magazine.

"Frankie. You're late." His accent sounded like he was far from home.

If my dad was worried about it, he didn't show it. "Ilya, this is my son Peté. I had to pick him up and there was traffic. Is now okay, or should I come back later?"

Ilya looked at me and smiled without showing his teeth. "No, this is fine. I'm glad you brought Peté. I did not know you are family man. Please come in." He left the door open and walked inside.

Dad went in first. My stomach felt like it was climbing out of my mouth. I wanted to tell my father I didn't like this man. I wanted to tell him let's go home. I wanted Mom. But I wanted more for Dad not to call me a pussy, so I followed him into the living room.

There was no cigarette smoke in the air. I didn't smell old grease or food. No hint of incense or flowers. Instead, it smelled like a can of Lysol and bucket of bleach. No sounds came from upstairs or next-door neighbors.

The tiles looked like a chessboard. Photographs of a beach hung on the walls; none had people in them. The sofas were made of black leather, and it was the first time I had seen a sofa that wasn't upholstered with fabric. Strange sculptures that looked like black snakes stood displayed on the end tables. He had a large TV, the biggest I had ever seen. The speakers next to it stood taller than the big screen and matched the couches.

Ilya gave me three remotes. "This one for sound. This one for TV. This one for cable. Okay?"

Dad said, "He's a smart kid. Good with gadgets and shit." He sat me down on the couch and said, "Now me and Ilya are going to be in the next room with the door closed. Talking business, you know. Just hang out, watch TV, and then we'll be on our way. All right?"

Ilya asked me, "Do you want some chips?"

Dad waved his hand. "No. Got an apple?"

Ilya went to the kitchen and ran water over an apple while I examined the remote controls.

Dad placed the washed apple in my hand and then left with Ilya to talk business. I was alone in the living room.

After some messing with the order of activation, I figured out how to turn on the TV, speakers, and cable. I was delighted at the first channel that came on. Ilya didn't just have basic cable; he had more than Marta. He had HBO.

I turned to the channel and found the middle of a comedy special was playing. An old white man with gray hair tied back in a ponytail stood on stage. He wore a simple black T-shirt and pants and talked about the seven words you couldn't say on TV: shit, piss, fuck, cunt, cocksucker, motherfucker, and tits. The TV crowd laughed.

The apple was still in my hand. I didn't want it, so I went back to the kitchen to put it away. Everything was spotless and new. This must be how Mom would want her kitchen to look if we had money. I didn't find the fruit bowl, so I left the apple on the counter. All the plates and dishes were so neatly stacked, they seemed to be more for decoration than use. I went back to the couch and finished watching the show.

The man cursed so eloquently, I was hypnotized. I knew what all the words he said meant but not in the combinations he used. The man seemed to me not only intelligent and honest but also having the courage to say what he thought. In my mind, this gave him power. The comedian took pleasure in pointing out the contradictions in life, culture, and government, and the crowd loved him for it. I laughed so hard my sides began to ache as if I were running far and fast, and then I cried.

George Carlin said so many things that had rhymed with my father in the car. Criminals and cops being sides of the same coin. Bullets were shaped like dicks for men to fuck other men to death. My mind reacted to the day's contradictions and their logic with laughter. It was the first time my young mind had contemplated the absurdity of the human condition. My laugh sounded to myself like the Joker, who I had heard cackle about the mad world countless times after school on the *Batman* animated series.

Dad and Ilya came out of their meeting. A strong smell of weed followed them out. Dad checked to make sure I was okay and shook me out of my laughing convulsions. I wiped my tears and he put his arms over me. He held a full-sized blunt in his hand. Ilya stood behind the couch and watched the last few jokes with us.

Dad laughed. "Ah, George Carlin. Funny man, my favorite comedian."

Ilya pretended to laugh without smiling.

The show ended with even more applause. Dad took this opportunity to get up and head to the door. I followed him. Ilya spoke no good-byes but watched us with his cold eyes. Dad returned the stare, and his eyes for a moment were just as cold and animal-looking as Ilya's. I noticed the bag we came with didn't leave with us. My father now carried a different bag.

The sun was long gone outside. I saw no stars. We drove out and headed back toward Marta and our family.

I sat quietly. Dad didn't play any music. The dark road made him more attentive for police. We drove the speed limit the whole way.

When we pulled into Marta's condo, he cut the engine and, in the silence, said, "The goal is to get out of the U.S. I'm doing what I can to get us the money to buy fake passports and get to Argentina."

Telling me was his way of apologizing for bringing me along to a drug deal. I learned later that my participation in his errands was key. In criminal circles, bringing your son along is a sign that you intend no harm and want to be serious and just do business.

I unbuckled. "Okay." I was relieved to have a destination. We weren't going to run forever. I would return to a life with school, friends, grow up, and have a career. In Argentina.

4

A few days after Dad had drugs to move, we left Marta's condo. Her good-bye to me felt sincere—her eyes filled with tears and her words spoke of benedictions that only Cuban mothers knew.

Before we left, Dad sat down with us in the living room and told us our cover story. His stolen identity was Joe Cuesta, my mother's first husband. He had acquired his Social Security number from old papers from Mom and with the help of his connections had produced a fake temporary driver's license and tags. He instructed further, "If anyone asks, we're just visiting family after Hurricane Andrew and ain't staying long."

We drove away in a cream white Mercedes-Benz 300-Class sedan. I didn't ask what happened to the Honda or where we were going. I just hoped the next place would be some criminal's apartment where we could get fake passports and run to our next lives.

On the road I noticed there were fewer construction crews working on power lines and the National Guard soldiers had disappeared. Life in Miami had returned to normal. After ten radio songs, I began to recognize the surroundings.

We passed the Farm Store where Memé had committed her first shoplift—the same one where I had bought baseball cards, packaged with stale gum sticks, and had paid with couch change. No one spoke a word when we arrived at the walled community of the Bleau Fontaine condominiums, but we knew this place. It was

my old neighborhood, where my family had lived until moving to
Louisiana a year ago.

In these relatively secure streets in the Miami suburbs, we had a
broken home. I played and stayed outside as much as possible and
avoided the needles, burned spoons, dangerous men, and Mom.
Even now I always feel safer in the streets and on the move, rather
than inside my own home.

The Bleau Fontaine gatehouse stood empty. The hurricane
hadn't damaged anything; even the Spanish tiles were still in place
and bright orange. The community was a collection of two-story
buildings, each one with eight condos of varying square footage and
white walls with false stucco. Every grass field had live oaks and
eucalyptus trees providing shade. I kept silent as my father drove
us through the streets where my friends and I had tossed footballs,
the empty parking spot where I'd gotten my first black eye, and the
field where I'd won my first fistfight.

I had thought the reason we were here was to see my aunt Odalis,
who lived nearby, but I had doubts she would willingly harbor a
fugitive. Also, she hated my father.

We passed our old broken home and parked in the building across
from it. Dad turned the engine off and whipped his head back toward
me and the other kids. "Let's go."

I wanted to obey but couldn't help to ask, "Where?"

Dad busied himself with papers from the glove box. Mom smiled
and reached back to stroke my hair. "We're going to stay at Dolores's."

Memé giggled and squirmed. She was impatient to get out of
the car and pushed me out. I checked myself from lashing out and
swallowed the hurtful names, like fat bitch or stupid cunt.

I moved out of the car and helped Chiní and Peewee out. Dad
watched me and did a double wink, the way he expressed approval.

I understood Memé's excitement. Dolores's daughter, Juanita,
was her longtime playmate. While I roamed these streets playing

war on asphalt, she and Juanita walked around the block or played with dolls at her place. They'd gather in corners and talk. God only knows what little girls talk about among themselves, but they both looked at me like I was trash whenever I got close enough to find out.

We left our bags in the Mercedes. Dolores's building was identical to ours in the condo complex, right down to the fire extinguisher placement and exit signs. Each had outdoor courtyards with a garden of smooth white stones and Spanish shrubs in the center. Dolores lived upstairs in one of the larger condo models.

Going up, I held on to the rails my friends used to slide down. I planned to go and tell them I was back after we were settled. Dad knocked on Dolores's door.

A melodic voice with a thick Spanish accent answered, "Hello, my darlings." Dolores wore full makeup, jeans so tight it looked like they might have been spray-painted on, and a blouse that was only appropriate at a nightclub. It wasn't noon yet.

I knew who she was and that she'd partied with Mom, but I had never really seen her before. She was Venezuelan and held the door open with a smile that confused me because it appeared warm but felt dangerous. In my prepubescent mind, naturally uncomfortable with sex, grew unfamiliar feelings. I didn't know what the word *voluptuous* meant until then. My hands hid deep in my pockets, and I kept from meeting her eyes.

Thick perfume like a chemical weapon filled my lungs. I couldn't understand the desire in my body, but her scent made me feel like this woman was bad. Years later I understood after a wise former prostitute in recovery told me, "If it smells like cologne, leave it alone."

Dad grabbed me by the shoulder. "Come with me to get the bags while the little ones settle in with Mom."

When we were outside and pulling plastic grocery bags filled with clothes out of the trunk, I asked Dad if I could tell him something.

He fixed a glare on me. "Peté, don't tell me you're hungry."

I shook my head. "Dad, I don't like the way Dolores smells."

"Yeah, she does lay it on too thick for me." Dad hocked a wad of spit, the color of it a shade of off-white and closer to the color of old money. He held a bag with the JCPenney logo, and I knew that held another bag with the drugs.

"No, I mean, I don't like her. I think she's a bad person."

We stood there holding everything we owned and stared at each other. Finally, Dad checked around for people looking and smiled. "You can tell by her scent?"

I shrugged. Dad said, "Don't shrug like you're some sorry and confused thing. You said you know she's a bad person because of how she smells. Yes, or no?"

"I'm sorry." I thought he was mad at me, and I stared at his New Balance sneakers. The left shoe had a thicker sole. Multiple knee injuries had shortened that leg.

Dad slammed the trunk closed. "What did I tell you about being sorry?"

I looked up at him and felt like I was staring straight up at the sky, even though I wasn't much shorter than him. "Yes. Because of the way she smells."

When he said nothing right away, I figured the conversation was over and I started going back to the condo with the bags.

Then Dad laughed. "You're not wrong. If you can tell that by the way she smells, you have great instincts."

I realized I had been holding my breath. "You're not mad?"

"No, son. Your instincts—man, never ignore them. Yes, your nose is perceptive."

The bags began to feel as if they were filled with concrete blocks. "So, shouldn't we leave?"

Dad shook his head. My hands felt as if they were coming apart; the plastic handle left marks in my soft hands.

Dad slouched with the weight of the bags but kept them up. "We have no choice. We'll be here only as long as we have to. Keep an eye out for your siblings. Keep them safe. Can you do that for me?"

I couldn't take care of myself, let alone the three other children. Dad continuously questioned my upcoming manhood and criticized my lack of useful abilities, so I had no idea why he would entrust this to me, but I couldn't say no. "I'll try."

"No," Dad barked.

I held my breath again. I started counting the number of cracks in the pavement—anything to distract my attention from the putdowns and disgust he had been beating me down with since we'd been reunited.

"Hey." Dad's voice got soft. "Do or do not. There is no try. You saw *Star Wars*, right?"

I hadn't known he knew that line. Maybe he had seen it in prison or during one of the years he was a free man. I put it in the back of my mind, a question for another time. "Okay, Yoda."

Dad barked a laugh. "Pick up the bags. You are not a Jedi yet."

I wrapped my hands around the handle and grunted pathetically. "I'm more into *Star Trek*."

Dad said, "I love you."

"I know."

Dad laughed. "That was such a dope scene. Princess Leia said that shit to Han, and he told that bitch, 'Yeah, I know.'"

We walked back to the building stairs. Dad commanded me to sprint up the steps. I didn't mind; my feet felt lighter after our moment of science fiction banter and the approval of my one useful trait: instinct. By the time I crossed Dolores's doorway, a cramp had hit me on my chunky legs and stitches began to stab my fleshy ribs.

Peewee sat on Mom's lap while she chatted with Dolores on her sofa, which looked like it came from the same furniture store where the Russian wolf-man, Ilya, bought his stuff. Dolores's home had as many portraits of Marilyn Monroe as a Catholic church has of Jesus and Mary. The air smelled like incense and hair spray.

Juanita showed Memé and Chiní her new Barbie dolls by the coffee table. She was the same age as Memé and disliked me, often speaking the same insults Memé used on me. When I talked back to her with the same insults I used on Memé, she grew defensive instead of fighting back. She wore loose clothes to conceal her chubby body and had eyebrows that were bushy; she appeared as plain as Dolores was stunning, and next to each other in the same room it was hard to believe they were related. Looking back, I understand Dolores's brutal critiques of her appearance had forced Juanita to develop an attitude that distrusted compliments and held everyone to her mother's standard of beauty. Her insecurities were not too different from mine.

The second-story condos had a loft. Dad put his load down and sat on the sofa. "Take care of it," he ordered. With his knee, he avoided stairs as often as he could.

Dolores dismissed me with her hands, as if she were sweeping dirt. "*Chico*, put all that upstairs and come back down."

Taking as many bags as possible, I completed the task in three trips. When I set down Mom's large makeup bag, I saw that under a photo of Madonna looking like Marilyn there sat a desk with a PC and monitor.

I'd never seen a computer outside of school. The all-in-one Apple Macintosh machines purchased by the Miami–Dade County Public Schools didn't allow for much exploration outside of the handful of educational applications like *Oregon Trail* and *Where in the World Is Carmen San Diego*. I'd wanted to know more about these machines since I'd seen one on TV. I'd watched all the cartoons with sentient robots and adored *Star Trek: The Next Generation*'s android character, Data. On those shows, computers seemed to have all the answers. My elementary school teachers had once told my mother I had demonstrated a knack for understanding all the abstract ways that computers worked. They encouraged me to apply for a county school program focusing on tech, but we moved and were too poor to have a computer anyway.

Under the sexual gaze of Madonna, I learned the PC model: IBM PS 1. The color of the plastic case reminded me of the beige and gray paint at the federal correctional facilities. The DOS 4.01 operating system ran off a ROM disk. It had a 10-megahertz processor and packed 1 megabyte of memory. Mom called for me. Excited like the fat-kid-I-was in a candy store, I ran down the carpeted steps.

The girls were nowhere to be seen, and Peewee now bounced on Dad's good knee. My mother and Dolores sat on either side of him. After catching my breath, I pointed back up to the loft. "Dad, there's a computer here."

"So what?" Dad stopped playing with Peewee and kept his face impassive, as if telling me sci-fi playtime ended at the parking lot.

"Leave him alone." Dolores's spoke with her eyes half closed, and she reached over and rubbed his shoulder. Her lips pouted. "If you want to play with that thing, go ahead. I don't use it." Again, she dismissed me as if I were a peasant. She had a ring on every finger, and her nails were tinted bright red. Again, parts of me fired up and the rest feared her.

In the first few days, Mom and Dad spent most of their time in Dolores's room behind closed doors. Memé and Chiní slept in Juanita's room and played with her dolls or dressed up like her mom. Peewee and I slept upstairs in the loft by the computer.

Dolores had cable, just like Marta did, so Peewee and I watched cartoons all day. Outside I heard my old friends play tackle football on the asphalt or ride bicycles up and down the parking spaces like BMX amateurs.

I grew restless staying indoors. TV, computer, and Juanita's Super Nintendo could only provide so much stimulus. The time had come to be away and avoid what the grown-ups did behind closed doors. When I could take no more, I woke up early, did my exercises, got dressed, put my shoes on, and waited for Dad outside of Dolores's room.

In the afternoon, he limped out to the kitchen in his shorts. The scars on his knees seemed more alive when he wasn't sober. His hands darted around the fridge and pulled out a bottle of grapefruit juice. He set a tall glass down on the countertop so hard I flinched. To my surprise the glass didn't shatter in a million pieces. A little at a time he filled it, the whites of his eyes redder than the juice.

"Dad," I said.

He stopped pouring. "Don't come to me like a bitch. Just say what you're going to say." He pointed to the juice bottle. "Want some?"

I hated grapefruit juice; the sour fruit had always made the inside of my mouth taste like acetone for hours afterward. "No. Can I go outside and see my friends?"

Dad resumed pouring the juice. He stopped after the glass was half full and lifted the bottle a handspan higher. "What do you think will happen when I pour this high?"

I'd prepared all morning for this talk, to recite to Dad the story I'd tell my friends and repeat our vow of silence about our run from the law. But when he was high, I had no idea if he spoke in metaphor or was being simply playful. "What?"

Dad shook his head. "Is something wrong with your hearing?" The juice poured down and met the surface in the glass like a waterfall. Some of the liquid splashed on the countertop. Dad stopped pouring at about two-thirds full and raised the bottle even higher. "What do you think will happen now?"

I scanned the kitchen for answers and searched his face for a clue to this game.

"Stop looking like there's a camera filming you, son."

I met his eyes like he always told me to do and felt small, about the size of an ant. "I don't know. I think you'll make a mess."

"Why?" Dad's mouth worked every muscle into the word.

"It splashes harder the higher it goes."

Dad set the juice down and slapped the countertop hard with both hands. "Yes." His palms were pink. "The farther it is, the more time it has to accelerate because of gravity. The more it accelerates over time, the more velocity it gains. Therefore, it has more force."

I'd seen many episodes of *Star Trek* where actors playing engineers, scientists, and navigators had used those words: acceleration, velocity, gravity, force. "Okay."

He gulped the juice, his Adam's apple bobbing up and down with a lot of this force he mentioned. "It's physics. Don't they teach you that in school?"

"No." My sixth-grade math teacher hadn't gotten us to pre-algebra yet. I hadn't been in a classroom for a month.

"No matter. You can learn this without them. You can teach yourself. I'll buy you a book on physics." He drained his glass. "I'll teach you about magnets too. You can make electricity with that knowledge. That'll come in handy after May 5, 2000. The world will end as we know it, and we will need people like you, son, with your mind."

He'd said the date the world would end, and I forgot everything else. The door outside to my friends might as well have been on the other side of the planet. "What is so important about that date?" Why he hadn't mentioned this before, I never knew. It seemed important to me to know the end was seven and a half years away.

"*5/5/2000: Ice, the Ultimate Disaster.* By Richard Noone. I'll buy you that too." Dad put his glass in the sink and the juice in the fridge. Without facing me, he explained how on that day the planets would align, causing the earth's magnetic poles to flip. This would lead to environmental disaster and a complete collapse of the world order.

My stomach felt like it had in the moments before a fistfight or when Mom had locked herself in her room and cried for days. None of those times compared to the amount of trouble coming my way. "How are we going to survive?"

Dad stumbled over and hugged me. "Insha Allah, son, we will. Allah will guide us as he always has. It will not be the end unless He wills it, of course."

At arm's length, Dad squinted and took my measure from head to sneakers. "You'll survive. I'll make sure you're ready. I want you to study to be an agricultural engineer. We're going to need those." He kissed my forehead. "You can play outside with your friends for now. Remember to tell them you're just visiting family and I'm Joe Cuesta."

Dad left me there in the kitchen and returned to the bedroom with Mom and Dolores. He hummed a swing jazz melody all his own.

Dolores's PC had a chess program, and for several days I hadn't been able to beat the computer. I sought out my father the next morning and waited until he came out of the bedroom to make coffee. I ran down the stairs from the loft and sat on the stool by the kitchen.

"Dad, I need help."

Dad opened the Café Bustelo and shook the can. The little serving spoon rattled inside. "You always need help. Be specific."

I rolled my eyes. He liked to throw out these comments, just like some teachers at school did when I'd ask, *Can I go to the bathroom?* and they'd reply with, *I don't know, can you?* He did this to remind me he disliked my lack of clarity with words. He always wanted me to be direct and as quick as possible, to get to the point. "I can't beat the computer at chess, and I need help winning."

He nodded and opened a drawer. "Let me finish here. Go upstairs and wait for me."

I ran up and sat down at the desk. I started a new game and drummed the desk with my fingers. I'd gotten used to the stink of Dolores's perfume and could only smell it when she got close. The large picture of Marilyn Monroe stared down from above the monitor. The photographer had snapped the picture just as she laughed, her mouth wide open and her eyes half closed. All the pictures Dolores had of her wore this expression. My father had told me she had her eyes like that in all her pictures because she was high all the time, and I thought then my parents must be high just as often as Marilyn.

My interest in chess had started three years earlier, when I was in the third grade, after I'd watched a game between Captain Kirk and Spock on an episode of *Star Trek* called "Where No Man Has Gone Before." They played with a three-dimensional chessboard, and I wanted to emulate these heroes. I later learned that the board on *Star Trek* was just a prop and had no rules, though the concept is based on a real variant of the game.

Dad had been in the corrections facility in Miami at the time, and on our next visit I had asked him if he knew how to play. He'd said yes and that he would teach me. The visiting area had a chess set, though missing some pieces, so we used Coke can tabs and water bottle caps to take their places. I learned all the different ways the pieces moved, and he taught me the four-move checkmate named the blitzkrieg, a phrase he'd told me was German and meant lightning war. He explained how to write notations for chess moves, and we played for months over mailed letters. He'd draw the board on the back of the paper each time so that I could understand.

My grandmother had noticed my interest, and the next Christmas she bought me a complete chess set. Dad frowned on these holiday gifts, but my grandmother ignored his religious wishes. I cried as soon as I tore away the gift wrapping. My grandmother thought I hadn't liked the present and promised to get me something else, but that wasn't the case. The tears came because I remembered a truth I had buried and pretended didn't exist: my father couldn't be here with me to play. I'd kept the set until my mother gave it away when we moved to Louisiana.

The coffee finished percolating, and Dad stirred the milk and sugar into the ceramic mugs so hard the clinking reached my ears. He yelled, "Lele and Dolores, come and get your coffee. I got somewhere to be."

His footsteps on the stairs were slow and measured, about one step a second. He grunted on the last one and let out a sigh. I pulled a spare chair next to me and he sat. "Okay, computers are not unbeatable. I had a friend, a master chess player, and the computer he played on caught fire."

"Who?"

He didn't name who this person was and kept on going. "Chess is a thinking man's game. A patient man's game. You have to think and keep an eye on the whole board. The whole board, Peté. You can't be careless!"

Careless and useless were the two things my father often named me, and sometimes he'd remind me not to worry about my personal failings because he'd make sure I would become careful and useful.

"Okay." I started the game on the PC by moving the white king's pawn two squares forward. The computer played the same move, and the fight for the center began.

Dad pointed at the screen. "The center—those four squares are key, Peté. If you own those, you own the board. Do you understand?"

"I know." I clicked on the queen's side knight to move it to protect my pawn.

Before I clicked the destination square, my father sighed. His breath reeked of cigarettes and coffee. "What are you doing?"

"Protecting the pawn."

He closed his eyes and shook his head; the combination emphasized his disappointment. "You are white. The initiative is yours. Why do you not attack the black pawn with king's side knight instead?"

"Because when I do that the computer attacks my pawn with his queen's pawn."

"You know this how?"

"It always happens."

"Always?"

"Well, most of the time. When I play white."

"Go ahead, son." He sat back and pointed to the keyboard and monitor.

The knight completed the move, and then the computer copied the move his knight made to defend its pawn. Not something I'd never seen, but not the move I'd expected.

"Well, grand master? What happened there?"

I shrugged and took my hands off the keyboard and mouse. "What should I have done?"

"You," my father leaned in close, "shouldn't have made these half-ass assumptions about what your opponent was going to do. Not this early in the game."

"But I thought . . ."

"You thought wrong. This here, the opening of the game, should be to develop your board."

"Aren't I supposed to think steps ahead?"

"If you can, but it's more important to follow through with your plan. If you make these wild guesses on the future, you'll only be reacting to the bullshit you fear. Develop your board."

"Okay, I'll try . . ."

"'Okay, I'll try.'" My father raised the pitch of his voice to repeat my words like Yoda.

"I'll do it."

He smiled. "Better."

I still didn't understand what he meant by developing the board, or opening theory in chess, but I thought maybe I could learn by watching. "Can you beat the computer?"

He sat straight up and smirked. He stroked his goatee and said, "Start the game over."

I got up, but he motioned me to stay put. He started as white. "Move my pawn like you did before."

I did so and the computer mirrored once again. From there my father played like I'd never seen him play before. I learned then he'd been holding back on me all those years and could've crushed me in every game we had played.

The game lasted maybe fifteen minutes. Dad lost. I don't remember how he lost, only that he laughed three moves before the end.

I asked, "What happened?"

He rubbed his hands. "Son, chess—like life—is a trade-off between position, time, and material. And just like life, it's possible to do everything right and still lose in the end."

I'd heard that line before, on *Star Trek*. "Really?"

"If Allah wishes it, yes."

I sighed every time his explanations mentioned Allah. "No, I mean you can play good and still lose?"

"When the greatest grand masters play, they draw more than they win."

"Wow."

"But!" Dad raised his finger to the sky. "They lose a lot less than they draw. Think about it." He stood, shook his bad leg to get the blood flowing again, and swayed a bit.

I got up, and he placed his hand on my shoulder to help regain his balance. He thanked me and turned to go back down to the bedroom, probably to get high. As he walked down the stairs, he turned and said, "Keep playing."

I told my neighborhood friends the story Dad wanted me to, and they accepted it without question. My father often said the hurricane, as an act of God, provided a better cover than anything he could've conceived and served as proof that Allah was, in fact, great.

During the morning, my friends went to school. I stayed indoors and experimented with Dolores's PC and listened closely to my father's apocalyptic lectures on preparedness. In the afternoon, my friends returned in a yellow school bus, and we played sports.

The kids played football or baseball on the asphalt, taking a time-out every time a car drove through or pulled into or out of a parking space. I didn't excel at these games. The teams chose me first for football because of my bulk and last for baseball because I sucked at hitting and catching a ball.

Still, I played. Running with the neighborhood kids and shouting back and forth with them about a life we knew nothing about felt great. After we grew bored with basic American sports, we started to play a game called burnball on the field against the wall separating the community from the outside street.

The neighborhood kids all thought we'd invented it together, but really it reminded me of a game Dad liked to play called handball. In my travels years later, I discovered almost every group of neighborhood kids had a version of this game. I even saw it played in the desert cities of Iraq.

Our neighborhood version of handball involved throwing a tennis ball against a wall and catching it after one bounce off the grass. The ground had been churned by years of playing, and even the crabgrass and weeds had a hard time growing, making the ball's flight path difficult to judge. If a kid in the path of the ball attempted and failed to catch it, he had to run and touch the wall. Meanwhile, another kid would pick up the dropped ball and throw it at the runner, the goal being to hit him hard before he reached the wall. If a kid got nailed three times this way, he had to lean against the wall and everyone took turns beaning him with the ball. We had no point system for the game and no rules for winning it. We just played until we got tired of it.

I think because of my size, I developed a good eye for knowing where the ball would head after hitting the wall and got really good at avoiding the hits.

One afternoon all the kids ran straight from the bus to the wall. I met them there, and we played for hours. In the past we'd add shoving to burnball to make catching harder. That day the game escalated into tackles.

Carlos, the only Puerto Rican boy among the Cuban kids, had just finished his turn against the wall. The game would reset after every kid spent time against the wall. As soon as Eric threw the ball, Carlos shoved Diego. I shoved the new neighborhood kid when he tried to catch. Then he tackled me, and it became part of the game.

Carlos declared players were only allowed to tackle just before the ball could be caught. A few rounds later no one had caught anything, and we were covered in sweat and caked in dirt. My skin itched from the small cuts earned from rolling in the field.

Nothing existed outside of the grass stains, laughter, and curses. I forgot the raid, the marshals, my father, and the end of the world. I don't know how much time passed like this, but maybe it lasted forever.

It ended when Diego and the new kid tackled me. They hit so hard, my feet left the ground and I tried to break my fall with my right hand. The fall dislocated my wrist.

Dad had once told me, "Pain is necessary for life, like water and air. It can make you puke. It can make you crazy. Yet you need it to be alive. Avoiding it is the greatest sin. You must meet it head on." He'd held a cigar stuffed with weed and smiled while he said, "You have no concept of real pain yet, my son."

Something somewhere inside my body snapped. I heard nothing, but I felt my jaw stretch open and knew I was screaming. The mouths of the kids standing over me were perfect Os, their eyes impossibly wide. They bolted away. I ran home crying like a madman and clutching my forearm.

If Dad was high when I came back to Dolores's place, he got sober really quick. I don't remember saying anything. He embraced me and, in the bathroom, set the bones back. Mom wasn't there, but all I wanted was him. He always knew what to do.

We spent the rest of the afternoon in the bathroom icing my wrist. It had swollen to the size of my thigh. Dad slapped my face every so often to keep me from passing out. In between the cold numbness and hot pain, Dad said the same thing over and over: "I have to teach you how to fall, son."

The next few days I spent watching cable TV while nursing my wrist. None of my friends came to check up on me, and I would watch them play outside from the window. They ignored my waves. My siblings stayed in Juanita's orbit, mostly ignoring me. Mom and Dolores left the room only to cook and eat.

Dad had started to leave the apartment every other day. He wore a fedora and black Ray-Bans and looked like a spy from James Bond movies. He'd return hours later, just before dark, and smoke cigarettes on the kitchen countertop where he'd given me my first physics lesson.

One day, he got tired of watching me grow bored and depressed. "Hey, useless. Why don't you read the Qur'an like I told you to?"

"I have." I'd read the holy book with the intent to impress him, but the texts confused me and I had no idea what the lessons in it meant to me.

"Recite the first *surah*." Dad took a deep drag from his Marlboro and waited.

I started to recite the opening line, the only one I had learned by heart, then screwed up the third line and stopped talking when Dad shook his head.

He said, "Okay, you only know the beginning. That's better than all nonbelievers. Now, those same two lines in Arabic, if you please."

I garbled the guttural language, and he slapped his hand on the countertop.

"Wrong. I know I told you to listen to the tapes in Arabic as well. Did you listen to them?" He waited for my answer and counted the seconds of silence by flicking his cigarette five times. "That's what I thought." He pointed to the empty stool across from the marble countertop.

I obeyed quickly, the way I thought a good son should, and sat on the stool with my busted arm cradled. The swelling had gone down, but it still felt sore.

Dad stared me down. "What garbage are you watching on TV? What is so much more important than learning about the word of Allah from the Prophet Mohammad, peace be upon him and his descendants?" His fingers didn't twitch, and his eyes didn't bounce around the room. He was sober.

"*Star Trek.*"

"What? Don't mumble."

"*Star Trek.*"

"Ah." He put out the cigarette with the kitchen faucet. "What was the episode about? Captain Kirk getting some green pussy?"

"No, it's not like that. You don't know it. Not yet." My words sounded like his but came from my lips.

"Relax, Peté. I will fuck you up."

"I'm sorry."

"I gotta get the sorry out of you." Dad rose from his chair and walked to the cabinet. He took out an espresso canister and a can of Café Bustelo. He turned the electric range to high. "What was the episode about?"

"It's stupid." I wondered when I'd stop hating the smell of coffee and decided never. It took a while, but by my thirties I got used to it and I drink at least a cup a day.

"You're sorry and ignorant. Truly, as a father I find this combination offensive, Peté." Dad packed the fine grounds into the espresso pot and set it on the range's coils that glowed red hot. "Come on, tell me. I'm interested in you, and what interests you concerns me." He sat down across from me again and waited.

Of course, I knew the episode's plot. If I watched it once, I knew it by heart. My favorite character was Captain Picard, not Kirk. I liked him because he had a large book of Shakespeare's works in his Ready Room, and he always read. In almost every episode, Picard quoted from a play I'd never seen or read, but it sounded profound and wise. I wanted to be like Picard: smart, compassionate, and in control.

In the episode I had last watched, Picard recited a line I liked but didn't understand.

"Dad, what does 'to be or not to be' mean?"

"Oh, son, that's a fantastic question." He spread his arms wide, as if to embrace the world. "'To be, or not to be? That is the question— Whether 'tis nobler in the mind to suffer the slings and arrows of outrageous fortune, or to take arms against a sea of troubles, and, by opposing, end them?'"

I sat up straighter. "Yeah, what does that mean?"

Dad snatched my hands and held them like we were in a séance. He squeezed me hard, and I flinched a little from the pain. "To be or not to be. Will you choose to be something or surrender and be nothing? Allah, the most beneficent and the most merciful, commands us to be!" He squeezed me more, until the pressure became too much.

Then I squeezed back, and it hurt less. "I still don't know what that means."

The espresso started to percolate. "Son, what it means is that we have to strive and fight to live. Truly live. Those are eloquent words. I am happy that you are interested in Shakespeare. I will get you those books."

He had yet to deliver to me the growing list of books he wanted me to read, but I liked hearing him talk about them. "Okay."

"But he is not as eloquent as the Prophet Mohammad, peace be upon him and his descendants. Turn off the TV and read the Qur'an for an hour. Every day read for an hour. I will quiz you, Peté, but life will test you." Dad released me and rushed to the stove. With his back turned to me, he insisted not only that I read the Qur'an daily but also its addendum, the Book of Knowledge, every week and listen to the audio tapes of the holy book in Arabic when I could.

I said, "Dad, when are we going to Argentina?"

He poured out coffee and milk into three mugs and turned. "Insha Allah, son, soon. I'm working on it. I've always chosen 'to be.'" Dad stirred with a small spoon. It made a rapid-fire staccato clinking. Some of the coffee spilled.

Dad walked back toward Dolores's room. I wanted to ask more. I wanted to know why he and Mom spent so much time in there, but I didn't. If he wanted me to know, I would.

"Read," he said before he turned the corner of the hallway and disappeared.

I'd been watching so much *Star Trek* that I'd begun to wonder how all the technology in the show functioned. I knew the technobabble spoken by the actors was fake, but I'd read in a magazine that Gene Roddenberry kept a scientific advisor on staff and that some of the fictional devices were based on real theories rather than plot necessity.

I sat on Dolores's couch and tried to get two refrigerator magnets to touch. My mind wandered. The way they attracted and repelled reminded me of how I'd seen tractor beams and deflector shields work on the show, and I thought maybe it was based on magnetism.

I had an idea that possibly that could be a way to fly without wings. I heard the crunch of a key working the front door and the dead-bolt snap open.

Dad walked in and locked the door behind him. Again wearing a fedora and Ray-Ban dark glasses. The light-colored slacks and bright teal polo he had on didn't quite match the dirty, dull gray New Balance sneakers. He'd just come back from an errand, and he never told me much more than that, not if he didn't want me to come along like he had back when we'd started this life on the run. He sat next to me and massaged his knee. "What are you up to, son?"

I lifted the magnets. One had a flag of Venezuela and the other a heart. "I was trying to make them touch." I elaborated on the idea from *Star Trek*.

"Ah, hmm." He took a deep breath. "Do you know about the invisible field those generate?"

"I've seen a picture at school."

He nodded. "Did you know it's very difficult to have the same poles touch?"

"Well, I thought that might be a way to push something away but not hard. And maybe one could float on top of the other, like flying without wings." I demonstrated as best as I could, getting them to hold the closer I brought my hands together, but the magnets kept slipping away from each other.

Dad put his hand out and I gave him the magnets. "The field around them isn't static, meaning it doesn't hold in place." He placed one of the magnets on the coffee table and tried to balance the other one on top, just like I had. "If you tie one of these on a string, the closer you bring it down, it's going to swing." He held the other magnet in his fingers and let the force move his hand as he brought it closer.

He got exactly what I'd been thinking. "How do you make magnets stronger?"

"You can make magnets using electricity, and the more electricity you use, the stronger the magnetism." He placed the magnet down and stroked his goatee. "Why?"

I bounced up to the edge of the couch and picked up the magnets. "What if you can use the field to move something on top? Like a car? Like, what if the streets were made of magnets and cars could float on top?"

I never stopped to consider the downsides of having a magnetically charged surfaces, or the amount of power required to generate the field, but the idea carried me away. Years later, and after more science education, I'd realize how impractical magnet-driven cars would be in the real world. However, I'd stumbled into how maglev trains and railguns worked and the many other uses of electromagnetism, thanks to *Star Trek*.

He placed his arm around my shoulders and squeezed. "You're going to be an engineer, I know it. You're going to help rebuild the world after 5/5/2000. I love you."

I lived for those kind words. I blushed and shrugged. I know some fathers tell their sons they're proud of them, but mine didn't. Instead, he said I'd help save the world.

He kissed my head and got up. He hummed and walked to Dolores's room and shut the door behind him.

We stayed at the Bleau Fontaine for so long that I'd sometimes forget we were on the run. In the last weeks of October, Dolores and her daughter had left to visit family in Venezuela. She'd said we could stay as long as we needed, and I began to feel like this could be our home.

Against my father's wishes we celebrated Halloween. He'd said it was a pagan holiday and anti-Islamic, but Mom persuaded him to let us have our fun. He agreed so long as our costumes weren't blasphemous. I dressed up as Mr. Spock. I can't remember my brother's and sisters' costumes, but I know we had fun doing trick or treat in the neighborhood like we had been doing before for years.

My wrist healed, and I returned to playing outside with my friends but avoided burnball. I read everything my father put in front of me, and my vocabulary expanded. I learned the word *complacent*, and he labeled me that often. I don't think he knew it applied to the rest of the family, but we were happy.

On a lazy November afternoon, my friends and I played tag football on the street. I got picked last for this kind of game because my size meant nothing without the violent tackles, and my catching skills had gotten worse after my wrist injury.

Just after halftime, Memé ran out of Dolores's building and screamed my name from the sidewalk that was our sideline. I asked for a time-out and jogged toward her. She crooked her finger to bring me in close. She scrunched up her nose at me and whispered, "Dad said to get you. Said come home. Now." She stank of Dolores's perfume.

"What did I do wrong?" Dad had given me a time to be home, and as long as I held to that schedule, there were no problems. He'd never sent anyone to get me before.

Memé ignored me and turned back to the apartment. I followed.

I took my shoes off outside the door and brushed away the dirt and grass on my clothes. The A/C kept the inside temperature below 70 degrees, and it felt like my sweat froze into a sheet of ice. As usual, the house smelled of perfume, coffee, cigarettes, and weed.

Chiní and Peewee sat on the sofa watching *Aladdin*. Memé grabbed my bad hand and took me to Dolores's bedroom. The decorations matched every piece of furniture in the living room.

Mom and Dad sat on opposite sides of the bed, backs to each other.

"Here he is," Memé said.

"I can see that for myself, Memé. Go be with your little brother and sister." Dad blew her a kiss and she left.

Mom rose and stepped quickly to close the door behind her. "What were you thinking, Peté?" Her voice trembled.

Gone the tranquil and happy mother of the last few months. Her eyes were puffy and red. Makeup and tears had run down her cheeks. She jerked her arms around the air, as if to keep from using them to strike me. The bracelets clinked and clanked, and I waited for the pain. This woman standing here was the mother I'd had before Dad had escaped and returned.

"It's okay, Lele." Dad continued to sit and watched her from the bed, his hands clasped around his little black book. He patted the spot on the bed next to him.

I went around Mom, putting more than an arm's distance between us to get to the bed. "I don't know. What did I do?"

Dad wrapped his arm around my shoulder. "You told someone about me." He spoke with more calm than usual, as if at peace with the world.

Mom hugged herself and screamed, "Eric's mom just came here. You know what she said?"

I understood then. Eric had been my best friend during the years I'd lived here. We hung out most days after playing and just talked about things. I had told him the truth a week ago because I'd needed to tell someone. He'd told me he would keep my secret. He had sworn to God. I felt foolish now.

Mom dropped to her knees in front of me and grabbed my face. "She said, 'If your child even looks at my son, I will call the cops.'"

My chest felt hollow. "I . . ." I stopped myself from saying sorry. "I thought I could trust him. He's my friend."

Dad sighed. "It's fine. I understand."

"How can you be calm, Eva?" Mom shouted. "He ruined everything." She howled and cursed in Spanish: *idiot, imbecile, little shit.*

I always hated when she got like this because it reminded me I could never do anything right and I made her unhappy.

"Calm down, woman." Dad leaned in and pressed his lips to my forehead.

His kiss made me cry as loud as my mother. I choked out the words, "I don't want you to leave." The snot streamed from my nose and Dad wiped it away with his fingers.

Dad shook me. "I can't have both of you lose your heads right now." He shook me again. "Hey. Real men don't cry, all right?"

I sobbed. "I thought I could trust him." I repeated it again and again.

Dad shook my head and grabbed my hair. "I've been betrayed before by more people closer to me than you know. At least you've learned a valuable lesson here. An expensive lesson, but important." He kissed me again. "I know you didn't mean me harm. Don't break our trust again."

When I grew older, my father told me a story about real friendship. He'd smart-mouthed the wrong inmate, an unfortunate habit he told me he had, and a fight broke out. Others joined in, and he was badly outnumbered and outmatched. Fists flew faster than he could talk his way out. His cellmate, Mingi, rushed to his side and caught as many punches aimed at my father's head as he could. They didn't win. Dad said they'd gotten their asses beat badly, and after the corrections officers broke up the brawl, he spent a few days in solitary. He said, "A true friend is someone who will fight by your side, not to help you win, but so that you wouldn't lose alone."

I hadn't learned that at eleven years old, and I believed anyone who said they were my friend was true. This was my mistake.

"Okay." My tears kept rolling. Mom too. She pulled her hair and paced.

"Stop swallowing your snot, Peté. You didn't lie to me or try and avoid the consequences. I'm proud of you." Dad stood and grabbed Mom in a bear hug. He shook her and kissed her hard. I looked away.

When they were done, Dad wiped her tears. "Get the kids packing, okay?"

Mom left the room and barked instructions.

"You too, Peté." Dad picked up the phone on the nightstand and thumbed through his little black book for a number.

5

My father didn't wait for dark to arrive. As soon as he finished making phone calls, we packed the Mercedes. Mom and Memé together dressed Chiní and Peewee for the road. The neighborhood kids had stopped playing outside and had left the chewed-up Nerf football on the street. I didn't get to say good-bye to any of them.

We left Bleau Fontaine behind, and the fantasy of a normal life disappeared. Dad turned on the radio and tuned in a Spanish-language station. I didn't know where we were going. Peewee sat up front on Mom's lap, and I sat squeezed in between my sisters. I hadn't eaten in a while, but my stomach felt filled with shame.

For the first time in my life, I began to understand the motivations for suicide. In *Star Trek*, the honor-obsessed Klingons killed themselves to avoid bringing shame to their houses. The mistake of trusting our biggest secret to a friend had been entirely mine, and the family, my household, had to pay for my stupidity. It'd never occurred to me that my friend and I were just eleven-year-old kids; I believed I should've been better, smarter, and stronger, like Dad had told me to be. To be or not to be—Dad had said he would always choose to be.

Memé whispered in my ear, "Why did we leave?"

Dad hadn't told her what happened. It seemed to me best to say nothing. Memé accepted my silence for ignorance.

The roads became unfamiliar. Rush hour ended, and Mom changed the radio station to one that played pop music. We were still around Miami, but farther south. Heavy equipment and debris mounds sat at every other street corner, even though Hurricane Andrew had happened almost two months ago.

Dad turned down a boulevard and navigated a maze of houses. He stopped at every crossing and drove the speed limit. The homes here were built with different materials than the part of Miami I knew. The roofs had dark shingles instead of bright tiles, and they had aluminum siding instead of smooth stone or false stucco walls. They were identical to one another, except some had a different color combination or garage door type. Dad parked our car in front of one painted with lighter colors and a roll-up garage door.

The sun sat low in the sky behind a middle school across the street. Kids laughed from a playground nearby. We stepped out of the car and huddled together by the trunk.

Dad swiveled his head around. When he felt satisfied no one was paying attention to us, he opened the trunk. "We'll get our things later. Nobody says anything; I'm doing the talking." He held the bag of drugs and touched everyone's face. "Let's go."

The lawn had taller grass than the neighbors' yards, and the concrete walkway had weeds growing through the cracks. Dad ignored the doorbell and knocked. He had a knock pattern, like a login password for everyone he knew, but I'd never heard him use this rhythm before.

A barefoot old woman answered the door. She wore a *bata* like my grandmother, but the colors were faded and the fabric so wrinkled that the flowers printed on it looked dead. Her skin reminded me of papier-mâché projects from school. She spoke quickly, "Come in."

Dad and Mom entered first, and I followed them with my siblings. We stood close together like the herd of terrified cows I'd seen on a TV documentary about slaughterhouses. Stacks of newspapers, magazines, and books lined the walls. Bits of paper clumped around the moisture stains on the carpet. The damp air smelled like a wet dog, but nothing barked.

The old woman shuffled away without saying a further word and disappeared behind a wall of cardboard boxes.

A man with long, curly hair emerged from another corridor of junk. He wore thick glasses and had a mustache that matched his home. He looked like every criminal sketch I had seen on the news. His toes were gray. "Follow me."

Dad made no introductions and didn't greet him. I didn't want to know who this man and woman were. My father wore a calm expression, but I knew he looked that way when he was being deadly serious. I wanted to leave, but we were here because of me.

Mom picked Peewee up and carried him. Chiní buried her face on Mom's waist. Memé had the same expression as Dad. We did our best to avoid touching the mold on every surface. The man led us to a small room. I could tell they had just cleared it out for us because the carpet in the center still had the imprints of boxes and looked cleaner. Stacks of books and boxes covered these walls, and to left of the door sat a small black-and-white TV on an empty milk crate.

The man left without a word. Dad relaxed and bounced his head to a beat only he heard. "Okay, I'll get us set up. Everyone stays here." He turned to me before leaving. "I shall return."

Mom sang to Peewee. She hadn't spoken or even looked at me since we left Bleau Fontaine.

I turned on the TV and picked a station. I moved the antenna until a clear image appeared. Memé took over the channel surfing, but I didn't mind. She found the afternoon cartoons, the old ones I hadn't seen since we'd been watching cable television the last two months. The antenna needed to be adjusted every so often, and I made this my job.

We stood around watching TV until Dad returned. He carried the brand-new blanket he'd bought for picnics. He turned off the TV. "Move outta the way for a second." The pattern had bright flowers. Sharp creases crisscrossed like a grid, and it reminded me of a map. He said, "This is where we'll sleep."

Memé sat on the blanket and flattened the corners. "Where will we shower?"

"Behind a mountain of shit." Dad stood with his hands on hips. He sneered at every stack of paper, every box, and every stick of exposed and rotted wood. "Do you need to go right now?"

She shook her head.

Dad said, "Okay. I'll show you the bathroom later; it's close. We walked past it."

Memé took her shoes off and sat with her legs tucked under. She whispered, "Are they sick?"

Dad smiled and then crouched down to sit. He grunted every inch on the way down to the floor. "Yes." He stretched his left knee out and rubbed the scars around his ruined kneecap.

Mom sat Peewee on the blanket and told Chiní to take off her shoes and sit. "Eva, what's going on here? Who are these guys?"

I'd thought she knew everyone Dad knew.

Dad lay back on his elbows and ignored my mother. Peewee left her and crawled next to him. He stared at the wet spots on the ceiling. "Memé, the old lady, Elizabeth, she lost her husband long ago and raised her son, Eddie, all alone. I think they never got over their grief, and this is the result." He looked around and whispered a benediction in Arabic.

"Yeah, but how?" Memé pointed to all the hoarded items. "Who could use all this stuff? Why keep it? This is all garbage and gross. They're nasty . . ."

He lowered his voice and spoke hard and sharp, "Take pity on them. Don't judge."

Memé opened her mouth and her eyebrows bunched up. A snarl formed on her lips, but she said nothing after a moment. She sighed, and he reached for her hand, which he kissed.

They sat around him, and I stood apart. No one spoke for a while, not until Peewee licked Dad's cheek and they both laughed, and just like that, they played like we were at a playground and not the home of sick people.

Chiní moved to sit between Mom's legs. My mother ran her fingers through Chiní's hair. "How do you know these people?"

Dad said nothing and continued laughing and playing the licking game. My brother moved on over to play with Memé, and she let him get a few good ones on her cheek.

The smile on my father's face melted, and he turned to stare at me. I looked away. "Sit down, idiot."

I obeyed.

Mom braided Chiní's hair. She nudged Dad and asked her question again.

I sat on the picnic blanket as far as possible from everyone. I remembered when Dad had bought it; he'd said he wanted for us to bond on this picnic blanket over meals under a blue sky.

He said, "Eddie and I worked together a couple of times. He's got a lot of guns."

"What do you mean?" Mom's eyes went almost completely round.

Dad sat up. "He's got a lot of guns. That's all you need to know."

She grabbed his arm. "He's a gunrunner? Are we safe here?"

"Yes. We'll leave in a couple of days."

I hadn't known what my father meant about having a lot of guns, or running them, but that freaked Mom out, and I knew we were in a bad place. I could smell it.

Mom closed her eyes. "A couple of days, Eva." She stood and said she was going to the bathroom. Dad pointed the way for her, and Memé followed.

Chiní and Peewee played the licking game next to Dad. He said to me, "We'll go out to eat when Mom and Memé come back, okay?"

Chiní asked, "Can we get a Happy Meal?" Peewee perked up and screamed yes. He loved the small plastic toys that came with the meals.

"No. That food is not halal." He stood back up, and it occurred to me I hadn't seen him pray since we'd left Marta's. Chiní and Peewee continued to beg him to buy them the haram food. They hugged his legs, but my father said instead he'd get them both a coloring book, and they were happy with this compromise. Chiní and Peewee giggled as Dad kissed and tickled them.

I examined the magazines, books, and newspapers in the room. Some of the magazines were celebrity gossip, and many were from before I was born. The books were from authors I didn't know, and they had mold sticking the pages together. The newspapers were from different places, some in Spanish but most in English. Nothing had been organized in any way I could tell. The items seemed to have been placed throughout the room wherever they fit. I did pity Elizabeth and Eddie, but they scared me.

Mom returned with Memé. Her eyes were glazed and her expression happy, like the pictures of Marilyn Monroe at Dolores's condo.

Dad gently moved Chiní and Peewee back down to the blanket. "Peté, let's go to the car and get just the bare minimum."

We walked back through the maze of junk to the door. This house had been built with sadness and loss by a widow and her gunrunner son.

The sun had gone down, and a purple sky covered the neighborhood. I breathed outside so the wind would carry away the stink of rot. The air inside the house choked us, and it was my fault.

Dad popped open the trunk and turned to me. He put his hand on my chest. "It doesn't matter that you fucked up. It matters what you do afterward. Afterward." His finger pressed hard against where my heart sat protected in its cage. "Do you understand, son?"

"Okay."

"Stop being sorry. Stop being careless. Stop being this useless blob of sad." He clapped his hand on my shoulder hard, the same way he'd slapped my face at Dolores's to keep me from passing out. It seemed so long ago and in another world.

"You make it worse. You keep thinking about it, you make it worse." He took bags of clothes out of the trunk and slammed it shut. "Now, pick up your little brother's and sisters' bags and start being a fucking man."

I grabbed all the bags and did my best to copy the dead look in his eye. All I had to do was be numb.

"Now do you understand, son?"

I nodded.

"That's better."

6

Later that night Mom forgave me, and we hugged. Her embrace lifted the weight from my chest, and it felt as if she'd freed me from being buried alive.

We kept ourselves busy by watching TV, coloring, or drawing. I had started to read some of the books in the stacks, but none kept my attention. Dad left us only once to use a pay phone, and we never wandered outside of our room except to use the bathroom.

True to his word, we spent only two nights at Elizabeth and Eddie's house. We drove away before the sun rose, and everyone breathed easier. This time Dad announced our next destination. "We're going to stay just outside Fort Lauderdale in a friend's house."

I sat behind Mom and leaned my head against the window. I blew out hot breaths and drew spaceships on the fogged glass. I didn't know anyone around Fort Lauderdale.

Mom asked, "Which friend?"

Dad said, "No one you'd approve of."

I'd grown bored with his paranoia at the junk house. The six of us had spent the last two days practically sleeping on top of each other. I wanted to know more about Dad's plan to get to Argentina, but he deflected my questions or said "Insha Allah." I wanted to know about the fake passports and how they were made and what we'd do once we arrived in Buenos Aires. The more I questioned him, the meaner he got.

Memé asked, "Do they have kids?"

"It's empty," Dad said, adding, "and clean." He drove under the speed limit until daylight and then kept to the slow lane the rest of the way.

We arrived at a single-family home. The neighborhood looked kind of like the one with the hoarder gunrunner, but the houses here stood wider and grass grew taller.

Dad stopped the car on the driveway and got out. He walked hunched over, with stiff legs. He took a quick look around at the neighbors' yards and opened the garage. None of the bright noon sun got inside. He peered into the darkness and walked back to the car.

Dad drove us in, cut the car engine, and pulled the keys out of the ignition. "All right, soldiers, get your shit out of the trunk and get inside." He gave me the keys and singled out on the ring a large key in a darker shade of brass. He pointed to a door in the dark garage. "Open that with this. Help your brother and carry his things. Mom and I have to talk in private. Understand?"

"Yes."

Memé beat me to the question. "Why can't we stay here with you?"

Dad dropped his voice and leaned in so close to her that his chin touched her cheek. "Get out."

Memé got out and I followed. I grabbed Peewee by the hand, and he climbed down from Mom's lap. The garage smelled like sawdust and rusted screws. Tools and boxes sat neat and arrayed by size on wall hooks and shelves. Peewee and I shared a smile. Together we grabbed our bags. Memé and Chiní waited with their bags by the door to the house.

I turned the key and opened the door. The air smelled of disinfectant and pine. The lamps were turned off, but the windows let in enough light to see the big screen TV and sectional sofa that dominated the living room. I suspected this place belonged to Dad's Russian supplier, Ilya, but I never found out.

The girls rushed in to claim a room, and Peewee waited for me to pick ours. Mom and Dad sat in the car with the doors closed. They argued. Mom used her hands to point to Dad and the dashboard and her chest. He shook his head and kept using his right hand to wave her away. His left hand gripped the steering wheel so hard his knuckles got white.

Peewee tugged my hand. I closed the door and looked for our bed.

The next day, Dad sat on the couch and flipped through the Yellow Pages phone book to find a shoe store near us. He wore a T-shirt and a snug-fitting pair of shorts that didn't belong to him. The scars on his pale legs looked like the maps he'd shown me of the ocean floor. He'd pointed at the underwater mountains and insisted to me that ancient civilizations more advanced than ours had been swallowed by the sea.

My father slapped a page, laughed, and praised Allah. He'd found a New Balance store, in his opinion the best shoe brand. He immediately called to place an order for a specialized pair of shoes. He provided specifications for a left shoe with exact measurements in metric because he considered the US standard sizing inferior and lacking in precision. He asked the man on the phone to repeat his order twice, word for word, then hung up the phone and wore a smile for the rest of the day. The shoes he'd been provided with in prison, and had escaped with, were falling apart, and he required special shoes to walk properly since his left leg was shorter than his right.

Years before my birth, he had crashed his aircraft into the Caribbean Sea. No one had told me what had caused the crash, but I suspected he'd either been flying while high or exceeded the plane's carrying capacity with his cargo of drugs, possibly both.

Less than a year after my birth he was in another aircraft accident, again in the Caribbean Sea and carrying drugs. Years later, while out on parole, he got high and crashed a car (with drugs in the trunk) against a light pole. Every incident broke both his legs, but always the left one worse. He joked his legs were kept together with pins and screws rather than tendons and muscles. He had no left kneecap, just a lump of scars and deep trenches from repeated surgeries.

I liked the new house we stayed at. The memory of my mistake—trusting my best friend—had already faded and my father never spoke of it again. This house smelled better than the moldy hoarder one and the condo where Dolores's perfume polluted the air.

Mom and Dad spent more time with us. In the mornings and nights Dad prayed with Mom, and for the most part she looked the part of a pious woman for him. We read the Qur'an together, and then he gave sermons about the Prophet and the history of the Bedouin. I didn't understand everything he'd say, but it calmed me and always led me to a peaceful sleep.

Dad went to the grocery store on the second day. Before he left, he turned to me. "I shall return."

He brought back enough food to last a month. After all the junk we'd been eating the last few weeks, some of which Dad had said was haram, he insisted we cook all our meals at home.

One afternoon, he summoned me to the kitchen and placed his arms around my shoulders. "Peté, you're going to cook."

I swallowed the lump in my throat. "I don't know how." I feared getting cut, or burned, but most of all failing. "I might mess it up."

"Don't get weak on me. If you make a mistake, do it like a man." Dad pounded his chest. "I'll teach you." He turned to the fridge and grabbed ingredients.

Mom had cooked for us when I was younger, but she did so infrequently and often served quick, easy dinners like macaroni and cheese or pizza. Once, she was so strung out she'd started a fire in the kitchen and the firefighters had to come and put it out. I relied on the free breakfast and lunch from the public school system.

"I got kosher beef for hamburgers," Dad said and laid out a packaged pound and a half of ground meat on the wooden countertop. The red blood oozed through the plastic wrapping, staining the wood and pooling at the imperfections. It smelled like a penny.

"Is kosher halal?"

Dad said, "Kosher laws are equivalent to halal."

I asked, "If Jewish beliefs are so similar to Muslims', why do they fight so much on TV in Israel?"

He'd paused his breathing for a long time before answering, "War was something Allah, most beneficent and merciful, prescribed to mankind."

I didn't understand what he meant, but I didn't want to dwell on the disturbing images brought to me through cable news. Even today, after being in war, I still don't understand what he meant.

Dad ripped open the plastic and handed me salt, pepper, and garlic powder. "Cup your hand like this to measure how much of each spice to put in the meat." His hands were pale and the blood so bright it looked as if watercolors ran down his skin.

I did as he instructed and spilled some salt on the tile floor. "I'll clean it up."

He waved away the mistake. Dad had small hands, barely bigger than mine. I lumped the rest of the spices on the meat, and to me it appeared now to be covered in sand.

"Good. Now, get your fingers in there and mash it all together." He gestured with his fingers and drops of blood fell and mixed with the salt on the tile.

I hesitated.

He stabbed his short fingers into the meat. "You can't be afraid of getting your hands dirty. Men get their hands dirty, Peté, understand?"

I closed my eyes and followed his orders, partly to avoid disappointing him but mostly to stop him from telling me about how much he hated men who aren't really men.

"Good." He opened the drawer to get a sharp knife and began slicing an onion next to me.

The stink of onion and spices mixed with the coppery stink of meat, and I smiled. It didn't smell so bad all together, but my eyes began to water. "Dad, why do onions make you sad?"

"Wiping your dying father's ass is sad." He lifted the onion to his nose and took a deep sniff. His nose was mostly plastic from car crashes, bad airplane landings, and fistfights. I'd never seen what his real nose looked like, but Mom had said I had his nose. "This is just an irritant, and your eyes respond by tearing up." Tears welled up from his eyes, and I realized that I'd never seen him cry before, and it seemed strange that someone so strong could cry.

I asked, "Did your dad teach you how to cook too?" I kept my eyes away from the beef. Even though it began to smell better, the squishy consistency bothered me.

Dad stopped cutting. "No. I learned by cooking for my children when I was sixteen." He resumed cutting. The chops from the knife sounded harder and came faster. "I taught your mom how to cook. Did you know that?"

"Really?"

"Oh, yeah. She couldn't boil water when we first met." He tossed small pieces of onion on top of the beef. "Mix those in there."

On TV, all I'd seen had been women cooking. "How come Alle never taught her?"

Dad put the remaining half of the onion in the fridge. "Alle can cook, but it's Abo who really knows how to cook."

"And he never taught her?" After I had the onions mixed with the meat, the consistency reminded me of Play-Doh. I started making shapes like mountains and rivers.

Dad pulled a frying pan out of the cupboard behind us. "In her family the men cook."

"In yours too?"

Dad turned his back and set the frying pan on the stove at medium-high heat. He poured olive oil in it. "No. My mother cooked, but she was old when I was young, and I just figured out how to do it myself. Like a man."

"Oh."

"Oh indeed." He turned back to me and inspected my work. "That's enough. Now take a handful of the beef and flatten it in the palm of your hand to make the patty."

I made six misshapen wads of meat. Dad nudged me over and quickly fixed my shoddy work.

Dad pointed to the sink, and I washed my hands. His hands joined mine in the sink. "You did an okay job. You'll get better the more you do it."

"Okay." The soap smelled of lemon and carried away the blood and spices. I wondered what the food in his home country was like. "Are there hamburgers in Argentina?"

"In Argentina the beef is cheaper than the bread." Dad dried his hands with a towel and opened drawers until he found a spatula.

"Why is that?"

He handed me a silver spatula that had no stains or imperfections. "Everyone lives around Buenos Aires, but we have lots of land for raising cattle. And we have a strong gaucho tradition."

"Gaucho?"

"Like an American cowboy." Dad set one of the patties down, and the pan, which had been silently hot a moment before, erupted with noise like static.

He passed the spatula to me, and without instruction I moved to place the rest of the hamburgers in the sizzling oil just like he did.

"Were there any gauchos in your family?" Microscopic drops of hot oil burned my hands, and Dad hummed a song I didn't know.

Dad smiled. "Yes. I'm the gaucho." He cleaned up the prep area with a towel. "If you want to know who I am and what gauchos are about, read *Martín Fierro*, by José Hernández. I'll get you a copy, but you have to get better at Spanish."

"There are no translated copies?" I understood Spanish well enough, but I only knew how to ask for what I wanted. My tongue moved too slowly when I spoke, and the words came out with halts and mixed up with English sometimes. It embarrassed me to speak, so I preferred to memorize conversations heard on Spanish soap operas and do my best to mimic the actor's lines.

Peewee walked into the kitchen and stood beside Dad. Each had a big smile on his face. "No, because there are some things that can only be expressed in Spanish. You have to read it the way it's written." Dad bent down and licked Peewee on his cheek. My brother giggled and jumped up to get Dad on the forehead. "We're going to make the meat well done. When you see the blood rising through the meat, flip it over to the other side. Keep doing that until no blood comes through." Peewee left the kitchen to go play somewhere else.

I flipped the burgers like he said and watched the blood bubble up. "But you read the Qur'an in English."

Dad straightened up, and his face turned pink. Deep in my guts I knew he was angry because he looked the way animals looked on TV when they were ready to attack. "The difference between me and you, Peté: I will one day learn how to read Arabic on my own, and I will have to make you learn. You're lazy, and that's not all . . ."

I didn't understand what I'd done to offend him, but I knew asking him only added to my guilt. I grew bored and kept my eyes on the food while he listed my deficiencies. He finally stopped lecturing when the blood disappeared from the meat, and we finished cooking together in silence.

Dad practiced Islam for his whole life, and years later I deployed to Iraq four times. Neither of us learned to read Arabic.

A couple of nights later, as I watched an episode of *Star Trek*, a commercial advertised that the next show would be replaced by a presidential debate. I'd already learned from school that U.S. presidents got elected every four years, and the teacher in my Baton Rouge middle school had said 1992 was a very important election year. I asked Dad if we could stay up and watch it on the TV, and he agreed.

After *Star Trek* ended, my family gathered on the couch to watch the debate. Mom had never spoken a word about politicians to me before, and other than stories of the communist revolution in Cuba, no one in her family spoke of politics. That night's debate was the last before Americans went to the polls. George H. W. Bush, Bill Clinton, and Ross Perot stood behind podiums and smiled at the camera. They spoke about their positions, answered questions I couldn't comprehend, and sometimes talked over each other but not like the arguments I'd witnessed. I understood very little about taxation or domestic policy, and I understood their responses even less. They all sounded like they believed they could do good things, but none talked about how to do good things. I only understood this: none of the candidates gave straight answers. Naturally, I looked to my father for answers.

"What are taxes?" I moved to the floor next to Peewee. He played with an action figure Mom had bought him that day.

Dad held a matchbook and pack of cigarettes in his hands. "Taxes are the money the government collects for the common good, to pay for things like roads and schools." His skin had gotten paler in the last few days.

His answer made sense, but on TV it sounded like no one wanted taxes. "If it's for the good, then why don't people want to pay?"

He stared at his cigarette pack. Chiní and Mom sat together on the couch and waited for Dad's answer. He finally said, "Because no one believes the government will spend taxes for good things. Governments tend to get corrupt. What have I told you about power?" Memé moved to sit at Dad's feet. She tried to snatch his matches. Her small ten-year-old hands were fast, but his were quicker.

I said, "That it corrupts."

"Absolutely." Dad hissed at Memé to stop her game.

"Well, which of these are good guys?"

Memé crossed her arms and stared at her crossed legs. Dad shook his head. "None of them. They're all politicians and have been corrupt for decades. It's impossible to get to their level without being on the take."

"Ross Perot is an independent." I liked the word *independent* because of what I imagined it meant: self-sufficient. "He's not a politician."

Dad chuckled. "Him. Even worse, he's just rich." Memé got closer to him and fixed her eyes on the TV. He said, "Behind every great fortune is a great crime."

I believed him. How could I not? Dad had made millions of dollars as a criminal. To him, the only difference was he got caught by the law and Ross Perot hadn't.

The powerful old men in suits continued to fence words with the moderator and each other. My attention wandered to my brother and his toys. Mom brushed Chiní's hair. Only Dad paid attention to the debate. The more words the candidates spoke, the more he shook his head.

Mom kissed my father. He cleared his throat and spoke to us. "Okay, nobody turns around. Keep watching TV."

They had us keep our eyes on the TV every so often at hotels and other places, and I'd thought it was because they were going to do adult stuff children found uncomfortable—light things like making out or second base. I learned in fact they'd had us turn away so that we wouldn't see them shoot up heroin mixed with cocaine, also known as a speedball. I learned this fact from Memé, the one who never looked away, maybe because she never did what she was told or because she wanted to watch over Mom. I don't know and neither does she, but I wish she didn't know what they were doing because ten-year-old girls shouldn't know.

Memé turned around, made her move, and successfully snatched the matches from Dad's hands. She laughed. "Got you."

Dad smiled, but his eyes didn't. "I told you I'm not playing. Give me back my matches."

Memé shook her head and moved to stand. Dad's left hand squeezed her wrist and she dropped to the carpet.

"Last time. You will give me the matches." Dad had a look in his eyes I hadn't seen before. They were expressionless and his cheeks were bright. He drew his lips back briefly to bare his teeth, or maybe to smile.

Memé treated his threat as if it meant nothing to her. She never compromised in front of a crowd. She called his bluff. "No, and you're not taking it from me."

Dad grabbed her by the hair and yanked her head around hard. Still, Memé didn't return the matches. The sound of his palm striking her pink cheek silenced everyone; even the TV got quiet. Peewee held his toys, and his mouth hung open.

"Eva!" Mom sat up but said nothing else. Chiní looked away.

Tears ran down Memé's face. I'd never seen her cry like that before. Part of me thought she deserved to be humiliated after all her abusive behaviors, while the rest of me felt guilty for wanting to see her get slapped again.

She still hung on to the matches. Dad looked ready to slap her again, and at the slightest movement from his hand, Memé dropped the matches. Dad let go of her hair, and she ran into her room. She slammed the door shut.

"What was that?" Mom placed the silent Chiní on the carpet.

"What?" Dad hissed, his torso rounded like a pit bull ready to lock his jaws on a throat. Mom said nothing and simply stared at him. My father picked up the matches and walked to his room. Mom followed him and closed the door.

The night ended. Chiní went to the room with Memé. I turned off the TV and took my brother with me to bed.

My father had told us many times before, with his chest out and big smile, that he never hits his kids. He never talked about the slap again, and he and Memé acted like it had never happened.

A week after the presidential debate night, we loaded the entire family into the Mercedes and drove to the New Balance store. Dad parked a block away, and my mother got out to pick up his new custom-soled sneakers. He turned on the radio to pass the time, and I listened to REM sing about losing their religion and The Heights asking how to talk to an angel. Mom returned with the shoes, and my parents kissed with their tongues. Peewee and Chiní laughed, while Memé and I complained about how gross they were.

On the return to the hideout house, Dad parked at a hobby store and smiled back at us. "I'm going to treat you kids to something special."

The store easily fit any house I'd lived in and had everything from telescopes to flying model airplanes. Dad walked straight to the aisle with kites and bought one for each of us. In addition, he told us to get one thing we wanted as long as we could run with it. Peewee picked a die-cast airplane, Chiní grabbed three coloring books, Memé a watercolor art set, and I chose a model of the bridge of the USS *Enterprise* from the original *Star Trek* TV show.

At the checkout he said, "I loved flying kites when I was a kid and I want to show you how to fly them." None of us, except maybe Mom, knew how to fly kites, so we were excited, but all I could think about was building my model. We left the store and drove back with huge smiles all around.

After Dad pulled into the garage, my brother and sisters scattered to the corners of the living room to play with their new gifts. I set up on the table where we ate our meals.

I tore the shrink-wrap apart. The box had a picture of the completed model. The bridge crew posed exactly like they did in the show: Captain Kirk leaned forward and rested his chin on the command chair, Mr. Spock stood with his hands behind his back at the science station, Lieutenant Uhura turned toward the view screen with her hand on the communication earpiece, and so on. The kit came with paint but no tools or glue.

I asked Dad for help, and he managed to find an old bottle of Krazy Glue and an X-Acto knife in the garage. He drove a rusty nail through the Krazy Glue nozzle to clear out the clot of dried glue. He laid out old newspapers on the dinner table to protect it from paint.

He raised the X-Acto knife to his temple. "Careful with this." He passed it to me, handle first, and then gave me the glue. "Don't get it on your eyes or skin." He winked at me. "Take your time and do a good job on this. It wasn't cheap."

"I'll try."

He grinned. "Don't try, just do or do not." He walked back to his bedroom wearing his new shoes.

I spread the parts on the years-old *Sun Sentinel* pages. Over the headlines of political news and global crises, I cut and glued together *Star Trek*'s finest crew. Their stories filled my young and foolish mind with hope for the future. I believed compassion and ingenuity really could improve life for everyone. I loved that show, and I still do.

The Krazy Glue dried and hardened on my soft hands and coated my nails. The sharp corners of the bridge stations melted from my excessive squeezing, and the knees and elbows on the characters bulged.

I turned the model to look at it from different angles. My eye acted as the camera, and I'd already started writing episodes in my head. I placed the figures at different stations and decided to keep them unglued from the deck.

I set aside the model and unpackaged the paints and brush included in the set. There were only seven colors: white, red, blue, yellow, black, orange, and green. As soon as I opened them, I started painting. Unfortunately, since I hadn't allowed the glue to fully dry, the paintbrush quickly frayed, but it didn't stop me from finishing the job.

Dad had been napping and had come outside to get some water. He stopped at the table and called me over.

I felt my smile stretched from big ear to ear. The model sat on the table still drying, and I moved the newspaper around so Dad could see each side like I saw it. I talked about all the characters until I noticed he said nothing. "What's wrong?"

Dad's skin turned the same shade of red as before he'd slapped Memé. "What the fuck is this?"

I picked up the empty box and point to the label. "It's the bridge of the USS *Enterprise*."

Dad pointed to the box. "I know what that is." He picked up Kirk and dropped it back down on the newspaper. His fingers came away stained from the paint. "This is shit."

I knew no words to defend myself from him.

"Did you even try?" Dad lifted the bridge and all the crew fell to the ground. "You didn't even glue them down."

"I did my best."

"The fuck you did. This is your best?" Dad tossed the model down. None of the pieces broke off, but some of the chairs started to sag. "I wasted my money on you. This is not your best."

"That's not true." Those were the only words I mustered.

Dad ignored me. "Your best would have been this." He pointed to the example on the box. "This is how the best looks like. Pay attention, Peté."

I kept my face away from him, so he couldn't see me crying. I tried to read all the bad news on the newspaper, but I'd covered it all in bright paint and glue.

"This is garbage now. You ruined it and wasted my money." Dad tapped on the table hard. "This is sorry. This is sorry."

The rest of my family had gathered around us. Mom put her hand on Dad's shoulder. "Eva, leave him alone."

Dad shrugged her hand away. "When I was your age, I painted model airplanes and cars. I know what 'best' looks like. This is you not trying. This is carelessness, Peté. That's all you are. Careless. And useless."

I waited for him to tell me more about what I was, but Dad turned around and went back to his room. Mom followed. My siblings quietly moved away, and perhaps they too feared to attract his attention to their gifts.

I packed the model inside the box and wrapped it in a plastic bag. I tossed it next to all the other bags that held what I owned. Everything else went into the garbage can, and I never touched the model again.

Dad locked himself in his room over the next few days. Mom brought him food and water from the kitchen and stayed close to him.

We cooked and took care of ourselves while our parents were unavailable. I watched Bill Clinton win the presidential election, and I kept caught up with the newest episodes of *Star Trek: The Next Generation.* Peewee and I played with his toys, and sometimes we'd team up and play games with Memé and Chiní's Barbie dolls. We had had a lot of practice in this type of situation.

I stayed up late one night to watch TV by myself. From my parents' room I heard howling. It sounded different than the other noises I'd heard from them. I crept to the door to put my ear against the cold wood. A muffled voice spoke and sobbed.

Mom opened the door, and my stomach dropped. I jerked back like I'd been caught stealing. She quickly closed the door and kept her hand on the knob. She took a deep breath and reached out to hug me with her other arm.

I wrapped my arms around her and she felt smaller. "I'm sorry. I thought I heard something."

"It's okay, Peté." She rubbed my back.

There were no tears in her eyes. "Who was crying?"

She said, "Your father."

I didn't believe her at first. This was the man who had said real men don't cry. I asked her again.

"Yes. He's really sick right now. He's in a lot of pain. You know he has those bad knees, and some days he just has to lie down." She kissed the top of my head. "He'll been fine soon."

Mom walked with me to the living room, and I sat back down on the couch. She went to the kitchen, and on her way back she carried a glass of water and a bag of almonds. "Don't stay up too late, *gordo*." She went back in the room, and I heard Dad sob before she closed the door.

I knew Dad had pain from his bad knees, but I'd never heard him cry because of it before. Years later, I brought up that night with my mother. She told me he had been going through heroin withdrawal. She said they'd been shooting up so much at Dolores's place that he became worried he'd get too addicted, too feebleminded to be able to continue evading the feds, so he detoxed himself to get his head straight. He'd kept reducing the amount of heroin he'd shoot up and then endured the discomfort—until he couldn't. I also found out from Memé about the time he'd slapped her. She had figured out what he had been doing and decided to help him by hiding all the matches. I can only imagine him, at the edge of his rope—our father's heroin-deprived nervous system had snapped and he broke one of the few rules he followed.

Not that he'd remain sober after that time. He'd take himself to the edge many times and pull back when he felt the habit had become too risky. The only thing that changed from that night forward was Memé no longer interfered with Dad, and he made a better effort to hide his pains.

7

Dad recovered from his self-inflicted detox the next day. I awoke that morning to find him packing the car with everything we had. He stopped to look at me head to toe.

Dad waved at me to come closer. He wrapped his arm around me. The air around him smelled like cocoa butter, cigarettes, and coffee. "Get ready to move, soldier. We're leaving as soon as the women and children wake up."

The sudden packing didn't bother me. That house meant nothing, and life on the run had begun to feel more like an adventure than survival. I quickly and quietly dressed in the room while my siblings still snored.

Dad directed his hand toward the piles of bags, and I carried them to the car trunk. "Good. Thank you."

The memory of my *Star Trek* model and his cruel words and actions seemed like it had happened to someone else far away. Moving and working alongside each other with purpose and a deadline healed whatever rift had formed over the two weeks we'd hid in this house.

Everyone else got up after we'd packed up everything but the food. I ate a quick breakfast while Mom got the little ones dressed for the road. Memé helped me load the last few bags with groceries, and we left the dishes in the sink. Then Dad drove us away.

I sat behind Dad. "Can I know where we're going?" I held in my hands a *Sci-Fi* magazine Mom had picked up for me at a grocery store a few days ago. The cover featured a pair of Klingons.

Dad turned on the radio, which had an Elton John song playing. "A house just outside Gainesville. I need help navigating. Do you know how to read a map?"

"Yes." I said it so loud everyone sat up straight. I'd become infatuated with navigation since *Star Trek* and all the histories of explorers I'd read. I used to make maps of places I invented and battlefields where my action figures could fight. I also loved being useful and showing off what I'd learned to prove to Dad I was good at something.

"'Yes,'" Memé mocked me, her voice pitched like a Disney princess's.

I hated when she repeated my words to suggest I sounded like a girl.

Before we could start a shouting match, Dad turned down the radio. "Enough. Lele, give him the map in the glove box."

From Mom's lap on the front seat, Peewee opened the latch, and she handed me a badly folded wad of paper. I opened the map all the way. It lacked the laminate that normally kept it clean, but I liked the feel of the paper.

"We're in Fort Lauderdale, right, Dad?" Chiní helped me by holding a corner. Memé kept her eyes out the window and did her best to ignore us.

Dad kept his eyes on the road. "Just go north and find I-75 and mile marker 205. Do you know which way is north?"

"North is always up on a map." The chart had all the spaghetti lines of roads in Florida. My eyes caught the blue-and-red shield with the number 75, and my finger followed it north to the green box with the number Dad wanted. "What then?"

"I'll tell you after we've cut west." Dad turned the radio up.

After Dad drove the Mercedes onto the interstate highway, I followed along with the mile markers and signs.

Mom slid into the CD player an Air Supply album she'd taken from Dolores. "I wanna listen to something else." She turned up the volume, and the song "Stronger than the Night" filled the car.

Dad exited the interstate. After going west for hours, we drove north again for so long we listened to the entire Air Supply album and a Duran Duran CD Mom had also picked up from Dolores.

According to the map, we drove along a state road surrounded by green parcels and tree symbols, and the view outside matched. Dad turned off the radio. We passed open fields with farms and enormous houses in the middle of big lots of grass that looked like they had just been mowed.

A full-grown dalmatian sat at the entrance to a long driveway that led to a house. The dog was as tall as the mailbox. Dad whistled. "That is a beautiful animal." My father and the dog watched one another as we drove past.

Dad turned left on a road that I couldn't find on the map. The asphalt had cracked from heat and rain. Trees lined the right side of the roadway. Dad slowed down to find the driveway of our next hideout. Fields of grass taller than me hid the entrance, and my father accidentally drove past it twice. He backed the car up and turned onto a dirt road that the grass had started to reclaim.

The grass grew shorter the farther up the drive we went, but tall wildflowers dominated the land. At the end of the trail stood a house, its windows covered in grime, and the siding had spots of mold. The property also had a barn nearby, and it looked as neglected as the rest of the property.

Dad stopped and parked the Mercedes in front of the door. "This is it." Rusted tools and planks of rotted wood surrounded the porch.

Grasshoppers as big as my hand jumped on the car, and I checked to make sure my window was rolled all the way up. I asked, "Whose house is this?"

Mom gave Dad a look and shook her head. Dad coughed and rolled down his window to spit phlegm, and I grew worried the bugs would jump in. "Remember Eddie and Elizabeth?"

"This is their house too?" Memé sighed.

"Oh, man." I already hated the house. I worried the inside was filled with garbage, moist books, and old newspapers just like Eddie and Elizabeth's home down in Miami.

"'Oh, man' what?" Dad turned to me. "I'm sorry, your highness, but the Waldorf Astoria didn't have any vacancies. Not enough room for a felon and his family on the run. The marshals booked the entire fucking floor." He opened the door, got out slowly, and slammed it closed.

We all followed him outside and grabbed our bags from the trunk. Dad fumbled with the keys and Mom had to help him.

I realize now that my father took every one of my complaints personally, even if the words were just my way of blowing off tension. Perhaps I gave voice to concerns he never wanted to confront, or maybe he cared a great deal about what I thought of him. In any case, he'd get furious and hurtful with me, and I never felt like it was deserved.

While he looked for the right key, I fantasized telling him off. I feared him, so I could do nothing but vent in my daydreams. Besides, even at that age I knew never to pick a fight I couldn't win. My mind kept coming back to Dolores's home in Bleau Fontaine. In my mind, he sat on her bed while I interrogated him. *I know I fucked up by telling Eric the truth, but we wouldn't have to live in a dump if you weren't a criminal. And what's wrong with telling the truth? Isn't that something you tell me to always do? Isn't that the virtue you are always telling me I have, honesty?*

Dad opened the door, and we entered the dark house. He flipped a switch, and most of the lights in the living room came on. Instead of stacks of junk piled to the ceiling, furniture sat neatly arranged, but it still stank of mold. The decor reminded me of older TV shows, like *All in the Family* or *Facts of Life*, with dark tones and browns. Everything had a thick layer of dust. The grasshoppers that had been living inside the house freaked out and jumped on the walls. I flinched every time their bodies made loud slaps where they landed.

Dad squeezed my shoulder. "Okay, let's get to work, soldier."

We started out by cleaning floors and moving furniture. The odor of bleach hung in the air for a few days, and then I got used to the smell. Dad bought new sheets and cutlery with some money he'd made on his last sale of drugs. The bag of drugs he carried had gotten much smaller in the last few weeks, but he'd picked up more prescription bottles of painkillers and antidepressants since the house in Fort Lauderdale. There were no phone lines here, so he'd drive to the nearest pay phone in town, about forty-five minutes away.

The place had no TVs. When I wasn't cleaning, I read books and magazines in the bedroom I shared with Peewee. He played on the floor with his few toys. Since we'd left Dolores's condo, my father hadn't been getting on my case for physical fitness. He hadn't had time between avoiding capture, detox, and finding a place to hide. That ended after we'd settled in Gainesville.

Dad barged into my bedroom while I read a *Star Trek* magazine article describing how transporter technology worked. "Son, drop and give me ten."

"What did I do?"

"Is something wrong with your hearing?"

Peewee left, and I got down on the floor and pushed. I couldn't do one, even on my knees like a girl. I kept trying but couldn't lift myself up off the old and stained hardwood floor.

"You've somehow gotten weaker, as weak as the day I came back to you." Dad gestured with his hands for me to get up. The smirk on his face was filled with disgust.

It took a while for my breathing to slow down. "I haven't been doing push-ups."

"Do you only do it if I tell you?"

If I said yes, I thought it'd piss him off. If I said no, he'd call me a liar. So instead of those two choices, I chose to shrug.

Dad looked at my tits and gut. "I'm not going to be here forever. You've got to get in the habit of doing it on your own. Initiative, Peté. That's what you need. You have no discipline."

Years after that, I decided to enlist in the Marine Corps. Veterans I knew had warned me about boot camp and the lean and mean drill instructors. When the bus dropped me and a few dozen teens off at Parris Island and those drill instructors barked and yelled abuses at us, I realized as soon as I stepped on the yellow footprints and stood at attention that I was more than prepared. I already knew their words because they were my father's words.

But in that house in Gainesville, on the run, I was just a boy and everything hurt and every word he spoke I took as gospel. I met my father's gaze briefly and said, "I know." I only knew how to agree with him.

He waited for me to say something more, but I just kept shrugging and I knew this pissed him off more than my excuses.

Dad pointed behind him. "Go outside and walk the driveway. All the way to the road and all the way back, over and over."

I got tired just thinking about walking. "What did I do wrong?" I rubbed my eyes so he wouldn't see me tearing up.

Dad's voice boomed throughout the house. "This isn't about what's wrong. This is about how much I love you."

Mom asked what was happening from across the house, but he ignored her. "Everyone else would leave you weak, fat, and ill equipped for life. Your mom, grandparents, and friends—they would be more than happy to keep you happy even if it meant you being a useless thing. A sorry creature I wouldn't even call a man." He waved his hands and mocked my shrugs.

I believed him; it made sense right then and there. No one else cared and everyone had allowed me to become soft—I believed this. I thought this was in fact love, and it hurt. Even today, after all these years, I still think my old man had a point.

"For how long should I walk?"

"Until I get tired of you sweating."

I walked and walked. Up and down, then down and up the gravel driveway. Bugs and tall grass surrounded me. Distance and tree lines obscured the neighbors' home; Dad had said the nearest one sat five acres away. The sun sat high in the sky and cooked my flabby body. My throat ached, but I didn't want to appear weak by asking Mom or Dad for water.

I kept myself distracted by rerunning episodes of *Star Trek* in my head, and then when that got old, I made up episodes. Everything around me seemed alien enough for my imagination, so I pictured scenes where Borg or Romulans ambushed the crew of the *Enterprise*. They'd have to run, get away from the danger, and find a place to hide and plan their ingenious escape. The barn next to the house seemed like a good place for the away team to hold out, but it was filled with darkness and ready to fall apart, and it probably contained exotic dangers. The open barn door looked more like the maw of a beast, and I was certain that if anyone peered too deeply, it'd attract the attention of the monsters living inside its depths. I have been many things over the years of my life and most of them I'm not sure of, but the one thing I do know is I'm without a doubt a dreamer.

Eventually reality dragged me back to my body. I began to chafe between my legs, what Memé called fat girl rash, and my shins felt as if they'd snap with one more step. Those pains were soon overcome by a stitch in my side; the stabbing kept rhythm with my breathing. So total was the discomfort, I ran out of fantasies. Then on the walk back up the driveway, I saw a go-cart.

I hadn't noticed it the first day; it had blended perfectly with all the trash lying around the property. I moved the old wood around it, careful not to nick my hands with rusted nails. My father had already shown me after I dislocated my wrist at Dolores's there would be no hospital trips if we got hurt.

The go-cart's wood frame felt dry and still looked solid. The aluminum wheels still had a coat of white paint, though the rubber tires had dry-rotted in the sun. I had no idea how old this go-cart was, but if it belonged to the hoarder son, who looked as old as my dad, it had been a long time since a child had played with it.

Dad opened the door and stepped outside. "What are you doing, soldier?"

"Nothing." I scratched my ankles and elbows, where the mosquitoes had been feasting on me.

Dad kicked at the go-cart tires with his custom New Balance sneakers, which he cleaned every day. "I used to build go-carts when I was a boy." Dad rolled the go-cart out and away from the junk. His pink hands turned red with the effort.

Then I knew what I wanted to do. "I want to fix it up and use it. I can roll down the driveway." The slope was gentle, but I thought it was enough to get the go-cart going fast.

He shook his head. "I used to race them with the other kids, and I'd sell mine to them after I'd win." Dad never missed an opportunity to compare our childhoods and demonstrate my limited ambition. With him it was always about my usefulness and ability to survive.

I sat in the go-cart. "I'll sell it to you then."

Dad laughed and spit. "No, son, I don't want your cart. Have your fun." He turned to the door and said, "Dinner is ready. Come inside."

—

Sleeping in a rural place took some getting used to. Instead of the constant sound of cars grinding on blacktop, music blaring, and neighbors arguing, the nights were filled with rustling tree branches and chirping insects. There were no streetlights or neon signs here either. I feared the dark, and my father knew it. *There is nothing to fear, son, but fear itself,* he'd repeat to me over and over, but never would it calm me. My mind couldn't comprehend the phrase; I only understood that I couldn't see without light and something bad lurked in the dark.

I survived the nights by covering my head with a sheet and never sleeping alone.

In this large house, the largest I had ever lived in up to that point in my life, I shared a room with Peewee, and we kept each other safe in the dark with my sheet-covering tactic.

One night, my sisters played on the living room floor with Peewee while I read a new copy of *Popular Science* on the couch. They decided to have a sleepover together with my little brother. No real reason—they just wanted to babysit and dress him up.

I knew if I slept alone, I'd have the light on, and Dad would call me out for wasting electricity (though I have no idea how it was paid; it certainly wasn't by him). He'd then finally start training me to be alone in the dark, one of the many skills he wanted me to have for survival.

I closed the magazine and sat on the floor next to Memé. The dark wood planks were rough to the touch. Dad had said we'd buff and finish it someday. I tapped Memé's shoulder. "How about we all have a sleepover in your room?"

She leaned back on her hands and regarded me from the side of her face. Our nonviolent interactions were more like careful negotiations, kind of like on some *Star Trek* episodes. I'd been told by all the adults in the family that brothers and sisters are supposed to be close friends, confidants, or partners in crime. Instead, Memé and I distrusted each other, and all attempts at peace were met with suspicion. We despised each other and didn't know why, but it had been our relationship since my first memories.

Memé stood and so did I. She looked at me down her nose, even though I stood much taller than her. "What for?"

Our father had spent hours to get us to behave like brother and sister. Last week he'd grown frustrated, either because she continued to scratch and hit me or because I never fought back with anything other than words. He tried to get us to respect each other, to understand our strengths and weaknesses. He stood us next to one another and said to me, "She is a killer. You are not."

I never got great at deception, and Memé could tell when I lied anyway. I spoke the truth and bared my throat, and, like a wolf, she accepted that as a sign of submission. "I don't want to sleep alone. I'm afraid of the dark."

She smiled. "Okay."

I followed Memé to her room, and the little ones did too. They played with Peewee, trying out different styles of clothes on him, and he enjoyed the attention. I lay on Memé's bed, a simple mattress on the floor, and continued to read my magazine. Later, as the night progressed, Dad came over to check in on us.

He stepped into the room and winked at each of us. His movements were fast and jerky. "What is happening here?" He pronounced each word like he was slapping playing cards down on a table. He liked to impersonate Bill Cosby when he was high.

Memé spoke for us. "We're having a sleepover."

He looked to the ceiling and considered this for a moment. He nodded his head. "Lights out in five. Brush your teeth and don't make me come back." He smiled and turned. Just before closing the door behind him, he said, "Give me ten, Peté."

Memé laughed, but I knew better than to start a fight in earshot of Dad. Besides, she knew I needed her to keep from being alone and in the dark. I pumped out ten push-ups, but sloppy ones—my head dipped down and my chest moved maybe an inch since my father wasn't watching me.

Afterward, we all went together to the bathroom to brush our teeth. We'd lost our toothbrushes between hideouts, so we brushed our teeth with toothpaste on our fingers.

I changed into my PJs—a big T-shirt and tighty-whities—and Memé made sure Peewee went to the bathroom before lying down so he wouldn't wet the bed.

Chiní and Peewee shared a bed, which meant I shared with Memé. The lights went out and the little ones went to sleep almost right away.

I stared at the dark ceiling.

Memé asked, "When do you think we'll get to Argentina?"

I considered her question. Dad never gave me any answer other than *Insha Allah, soon.* "I don't know."

She adjusted the covers and sighed. "Do you think we'll get caught?"

We'd never spoken to each other about anything serious. We'd only spoken words to fight one another.

I told her I didn't think about it. I had total faith in Dad's abilities, and it just wouldn't be fair if he went back to prison. Allah wouldn't let it happen, in my mind.

We asked each other questions like strangers getting to know each other. What's your favorite color? What one thing would you bring to a desert island? Why do you think the sky is blue?

Our night continued like this until we heard a cry and scream from across the house. I covered my head and feared that it was the federal marshals. My chest tightened, the way my father had told me sometimes happened when your body goes into fight or flight. We'd been found and our life as a family had ended. We held our breath and each other under the covers.

Then we heard the noise again, this time crying out my father's name. I recognized my mother's voice. Memé and I had listened to enough raunchy hip-hop songs from 2 Live Crew to know what sex sounded like.

We laughed so loud that Chiní and Peewee woke up. Dad heard us and yelled for us to go to sleep. I don't know why this seemed even more funny to us, but we howled with laughter together in the dark.

8

After a few weeks of forced walks and dietary restrictions back in place, I'd grown used to the routine and Dad didn't have to lecture me anymore. The Gainesville hideout had morphed into a home. Every night we sat down and ate dinner together. The table, simple and rough, looked as if it belonged in a public park. We played outside and slept in warm and comfortable beds, and my parents acted with kindness and affection for each other and us.

And we prayed together.

I wasn't old enough yet for obligatory prayers. The age of responsibility for a Muslim child begins with puberty, and that change was a few years off, but Dad of course insisted I read the Qur'an. He provided me with Islamic education through his lectures, whether he was stone cold sober or high as a kite.

One afternoon after a soup lunch, he told me and Memé to go to his bedroom so he could show us how to pray. My parents' room was on the opposite side of the house and twice the size of the one I shared with Peewee. The air inside smelled of sweet cigar smoke and cocoa butter. It was the cleanest room in the house, as no clothes lay on the floor and Mom's jewelry sat ordered and tidy on her dresser. On the wall Dad had hung a papyrus scroll that he'd told me had all the beautiful names of Allah written in Arabic.

He laid out his prayer rug in front of their king-size bed and announced the call to prayer in Arabic. Mom stood behind him, as is the custom when husband and wife pray. They both stood barefoot and oriented to *qibla*, the direction of Mecca. Their rugs were new, the vivid blue and black colors making the wood floors dull by comparison. Dad had told me the black cube image woven on them was called the Kaaba, the holiest place in Islam.

I'd seen Dad pray many times before, but I'd never seen Mom pray or wear a hijab. It stunned me to see her hair covered. I had no idea she owned one. The brightly patterned silk cloth framed her beautiful face, but I could tell it fit her poorly. My mother loved life and was a deeply spiritual woman, but she never became an obedient servant of Allah or any religion that dictated her conduct. She wore the covering and prayed for Dad, and, as I came to realize, so did I.

I sat next to Memé and listened. Dad turned his head to the right and called to the faithful; he repeated it again to his left. He set his head straight, faced forward, and began praying. I didn't understand any of it. He would tell me later that he always began his prayers with the first *surah* of the Qur'an and then recited another one he picked at random.

The sounds of his Arabic flowed poetically and melodically. After a few recitations he knelt down very slowly, careful of his old injuries, and prostrated himself. Mom copied his movements with more grace. His face rose from the floor and sang more of the prayer, and then he bowed again.

Memé cradled her face and never took her eyes off them. My eyelids grew heavy, and I lay down on the bed. As soon as my eyes closed, I floated in the air.

I dreamed the federal marshals no longer chased us. Each of us grew up and had children of our own, and Dad prayed a lullaby for his grandchildren every night before bed. There were no hardships, only joy in life.

Then I remembered my father had told me that no such existence was possible.

I woke up alone. Their tightly rolled prayer rugs sat in the corner. The lights were off, but the sun still shone. I stood in the spot they prayed, and the floorboards felt warm.

I heard Peewee and Chiní laughing in the living room. They played on the couch with toys—my sisters' Barbies and my *Star Trek* action figures. The sliding glass door to the backyard was open.

My parents sat outside with Memé on faded lawn furniture. Dad held a pistol, and he showed it off to my sister, his finger straight and off the trigger. He turned his head and waved me over with the barrel.

Fall had already arrived in Gainesville. We had evergreen trees all around our home, so there weren't any colored leaves like Dad had described to me once. The air felt cool enough that I would need a sweater if I wasn't under the sun.

I stood next to my father, and he said, "Have you ever fired a gun before?"

I didn't know what to say, so I shook my head and swallowed slowly so he wouldn't notice my Adam's apple bounce like a scared boy's should.

"Do you want to learn now?" Dad cocked his right eyebrow.

I gave the answer he wanted. "Yes." Mom smiled.

Dad reached into his pocket and pulled out a magazine full of cartridges. He slammed it in the pistol grip and racked the slide back. I flinched at the sound of metal and plastic slapping against each other. The crisp snap of a chambered round terrified me, and yet I wanted to know how it worked.

Memé got up and went to sit on Mom's lap. She didn't want to try it first. She didn't make a fuss about the attention on me. She feared the gun, just like I did.

Dad flipped the pistol and held it by the barrel. "Here."

I grabbed it by the grip, but Dad still held it. "Don't ever be careless with anything like this. Keep your finger off the trigger."

It felt more real, much more real, than the toy guns I'd grown up with. Deadly things felt more real than the not-deadly things. It had a silver upper and lower receiver and black plastic grips with a rough surface that bit into my palms.

I said, "Okay."

Dad let go of the weapon and impossibly it got much more real, and heavier. Weapons, like death, were heavy.

"This is a Colt Commander, .45 caliber, semiautomatic pistol," Dad said and stood up. He got behind me and gripped my shoulders. He squared me off to a pine tree a few yards away. "The safety is in the grip. Feel that little button in the meaty part of your palm?"

I didn't feel it, but I said yes.

He continued, "Okay, so the way you fire this is by squeezing the handle with the trigger." He massaged my shoulders to lessen the tension. "Go ahead and put your finger on the trigger. Shoot the tree."

I held out the pistol like I'd seen on TV. It was difficult to keep it up for long, so Dad held my arms a bit.

"I can do it," I said.

He backed off and I prepared to fire. Memé covered her ears.

And nothing happened. No boom like on TV, no crack like in real life when you're being shot at. I squeezed and pulled the trigger again, but still it didn't fire. I thought I had screwed up and said sorry to Dad, even though I knew how much he hated me saying so.

He smirked and rolled his eyes. "It's okay. Let me see that."

I handed the pistol back to him and he squared off at the tree. His movements were smooth and practiced. It seemed to me he was comfortable with the weight and reality of the weapon, and I envied him. I wanted to be that cool.

Then the gun didn't fire for him either.

"What's wrong with it?" Mom asked.

Dad laughed. "Son of a hoarding bitch sold me a busted pistol." We laughed too.

I caught my breath. "Can you fix it?"

Dad's smile disappeared and his eyebrows creased. "No." He ejected the magazine and moved the slide back to recover the chambered round. "Looks like we have a toy gun."

His face turned pink, and he spit a wad of phlegm. "Go play outside for a while, both of you. Peté, you should be fully rested after your nap; go for a walk."

I tried to say sorry about falling asleep during prayers, without saying sorry, but he dismissed it with a wave of the broken pistol. "It's natural to find peace in the word of Allah. This is a good sign." He smiled but didn't look at me. "Don't make me tell you again. Your mother and I need to talk in private."

Memé went inside and closed the sliding door. I walked around the house to the front yard. Before I got out of earshot, I heard Dad say, "Allah will take care of us."

"Hey, useless," Dad hollered for me from the kitchen, with one of my usual nicknames. I had also received a new one a few days earlier: unhappy.

I had spent the morning lying on my bed reading. "Coming!" I jumped over Peewee while he played with his toys on the bed we shared.

Memé and Chiní played with dolls in the living room. Mom sat at the dining table drinking coffee with milk and eating buttered toast. Dad leaned against the kitchen sink.

"Hey," he barked, "we're going to get into the habit of replying to my commands." He made a knife with his right hand. "At first 'yes, father,' but eventually 'yes, sir.' You understand?"

The thought of calling him "sir," my own father, felt cold. In my mind you only called cops "sir," and they were chasing us. "Yes, father."

"Good. Hey, listen, you're not going to lie around all day reading and feeding yourself. You got to help out around here." Dad pointed at the pile of dirty dishes in the sink.

I turned to my sisters. "What about them?"

"Don't worry about them. You're a man or hopefully you will be one day if I have anything to say about it." Dad picked up a coffee mug filled with pitch black coffee, no sugar or cream. "You got to learn how to clean up. You're going to have to get a job somewhere, and washing dishes at a restaurant is a good start. Wash these damn dishes."

He sat in the chair next to Mom, and I rummaged around the sink to find the sponge. Grease covered the hard green scrubber side, so I squeezed out a handful of detergent onto the yellow part. I ran the faucet and started on the biggest plate.

After finishing the second dish, Dad's chair made a grinding sound on the floor, and the unfinished wood on wood sounded like thunder. "What the fuck are you doing?"

"I'm doing the dishes like you told me to." I pointed at the pile of suds rising from the sink.

Dad moved like I had started a kitchen fire. He only moved fast when he was pissed. He shut off the faucet. "You're wasting water." He picked up the dish soap and held it to my face. "And the soap. Where did you learn to wash dishes?"

"Go easy on him, Eva." Mom sipped at her coffee. "No one ever showed him how to do it."

"No shit." Dad grabbed the largest cup from the sink and filled it with water. He snatched the sponge from my hands and squeezed the soap out of it and into the cup. "This isn't some city with a water utility. All we have here is a well, and we can't use up all the water. If we run out, we got to buy it from the store, and I'm not made of fucking money, son." He placed the cup on the countertop. "This is the only water you need."

I thought this was another one of his games. "That's not enough water for anything, Dad."

Dad shoved me over. "Look and learn, useless." He dipped the sponge into the cup and washed a plate. He turned on the water for one second to rinse away the soap and placed it on the drying rack. "That's it. Do it." He put the sponge in my hand again and waited for me.

"Okay."

"'Yes, father.'"

"Yes, father."

I did as he had done. "That can't possibly be clean, Dad."

"America has made my children wasteful. That's all you need. Trust me, no restaurant is going to want to keep you on payroll with the water bill you'd cause." He picked up a knife and handed it to me, handle first. "Put all the utensils in the cup and let them soak. By the time you're done with the cups and dishes, all you have to do is rinse them."

"Yes, Father." I continued to wash the dishes like he'd showed me.

He stood by my shoulder watching me. "I'm going to make sure you don't fuck this up, son."

"Okay."

"What?"

"Yes, father."

I finished the cups and the dishes and started on the knives.

He grabbed the hand that held the knives. "How is it that you think that's a good idea?"

I stopped washing and stared out the window in front of the sink. The go-cart had sat there for days untouched. "I'm doing it like you said. Father."

"You're washing the knife blade first. You're going to ruin the sponge and cut your hand. You want to meet the marshals at the hospital when I take you for surgery to fix your ruined hand?"

I flipped the knife to the dull edge and finished the rest. I kept checking the go-cart and decided afterward I'd start fixing it up.

Dad rubbed my shoulders. "Good job, son. See, this is a life skill that will serve you later. Do you want some coffee?"

"I don't like coffee."

"How about some tea?"

"I've never tried tea."

"I love tea, better than coffee. I'll make you a cup if you want."

Because he liked tea, now suddenly I did too. "Okay."

"Watch me make it so you can do it yourself next time. Okay?" Dad spoke softly.

He filled a pot with water and placed it on the gas stove. "First, you gotta boil the water. We should be boiling all the water here before we drink it."

"Why is that?" I'd already gulped several times from the tap after my afternoon walks. It had tasted like dirt, but I'd never worried about the water before.

"Don't worry, it won't kill you." Dad opened a cabinet and pulled out a tin can that had a Lipton label on it. "It's well water that's unfiltered and can fuck up your teeth." He smiled. "I grew up drinking well water."

His teeth were tan and mostly straight, only crooked at the bottom where the last two teeth met. Mom chimed in. "That's from cigarettes and coffee too."

"Yeah, yeah, woman. And fistfights." Dad waved her off.

"You got your nose from fights too, Eva," Mom shot back with a smile.

"It's okay. If I want to see my original nose, I can look at Peté." Dad winked at me and pinched the bridge of his nose. "This is all plastic surgery, son."

His nose looked nothing like mine. "How many times did you break it?"

"Oh shit, let me count the ways." He held up his hand and raised his index finger. "First time was in a car wreck when I was eighteen." He turned his head and stared into the pot. "Second time was during my first stint in prison. Third time was my first plane crash, then a couple more times in prison again." He ran out of fingers to count with his right hand and opened his fist. He feigned a punch at me, and I flinched. "I'd never hit you, Peté. I don't hit kids."

I looked at Memé playing with Chiní.

"That's a lot, Dad."

"Every man needs some scars." Dad laughed at his own platitudes.

"You were too pretty anyway." Mom blew him a kiss.

"I'm still pretty. Fuck you." He licked his lips.

"All right." Mom smiled and got up to kiss him, tongue and all. This display of affection made me feel uncomfortable. "Gross."

"You'll like it later, boy. The kind of kisses where you suck each other's fillings out." He cackled and groped Mom's ass.

I looked away and shook my head. "Come on."

The water had started to boil over. Mom and Dad disentangled from each other. "Open that tin and grab two tea bags." He removed the pot from the flame and turned off the heat.

The tea smelled solid and strong. Like coffee, it smelled earthy but somehow lighter and less aggressive. I gave Dad the two bags and he put away the tin.

He removed the pot from the fire and dropped the bags in the roiling water, leaving the strings hanging over the sides. A ring of crust had formed just above the water line. "What's that?"

Dad waved his hand away and shook his head. "The well water. You're going to have minerals and shit in there. It's okay, what doesn't kill you makes you fatter. By the way, after tea we're going outside."

"Yes, father."

"Good. Now you're getting it." He smiled and looked at his Rolex watch. "Now we just wait five minutes. Get a couple of cups from the cabinets and make sure they're clean and dry."

The kitchen cabinets had probably been white at one time, but now they had a color like nicotine yellow. The hinges had rusted, and they squeaked every time the doors were opened. Dad had told me the hinges were his trip wire to catch me trying to sneak food at night. Mom had put down paper towels under the dishes, the thin and porous paper separating our dishes from the filth. I grabbed two mugs.

The insides had been stained with coffee from who knows how many cups over the years. I washed them, careful to limit the water usage, and tried to scrub away the stains. I gave up when Dad said to hand him the cups.

He poured the tea from the pot and snapped his fingers. "Honey, get me honey."

I gave him the bear-shaped bottle that stood by the spice rack, and he spooned the golden contents into the cups. He stirred and handed me my cup.

"Drink it slow, it's hot."

I tipped back the dark liquid in small increments, and I breathed in the scent of hot honey. The tea reached my lips and burnt the tip of my tongue. Dad leaned on the counter and watched me while he sipped his. I took smaller sips and tasted the drink.

"Do you like it?"

It tasted sweet and spiced in an unfamiliar flavor. Inside my mouth my cheeks watered. "I do."

He smiled at Mom. "Good. I'll make you a cup every morning. Is it too sweet?"

"No, but it tastes funny. Is it normal for it to taste a little . . . ? I don't know. Sour?"

Dad drank and swished it in his mouth. He pounded the mug on the counter and gave a satisfied sigh. "Ah. That's the sulfur in the water. That's okay, you'll get used to it. But maybe next time we'll use bottled water."

We drank our tea standing in the kitchen. As soon as I finished my tea, he pointed to the door.

"Yes, father."

My father drove to the grocery store about once a week. He usually went alone, but this time he took Chiní and Peewee. Memé and Mom wanted to do girl stuff, so I worked on the go-cart. He told me to be ready to unload the food when he got home, and before he left he said, "I shall return."

They returned over an hour later; a lazy cloud of dirt trailed the car. The car pulled up to the house, and the smell of gasoline fumes overpowered the pine in the autumn air. Dad sprang out of the car faster than he usually did. He wore the same big smile as Chiní and Peewee.

I stood up and followed him to the trunk. Dad reached past the rice, beans, and beef to grab the kites he'd bought back in Fort Lauderdale. He'd stored the four kites, still new in their packaging, in the car trunk, forgotten by all of us.

Dad laughed and slapped his thigh. "After we finish putting away the groceries, meet me outside." He leaned the kites against the bumper and gestured to the food, the signal to get to work. "Chiní, go get Memé. Peewee, get Mom."

Dad's joy spread like a contagious disease. I gladly took on the task of offloading the groceries and putting them away in as few trips as I could manage.

By the time I had placed everything on the shelves or in the fridge, my family and their kites had been fully assembled, and they flew them around our house.

The grass grew as tall as my calves. Dad had threatened to assign the mowing of the entire property to me if I complained about any of my assignments. "Complaining accomplishes very little, son," he'd admonished. Then he'd recite a poem in Spanish, one his father had told to him. I only remember the last line: *It's when things go wrong that you must not quit.*

My little sisters' kites were pink and covered with flowers and butterflies. Peewee's had tiger stripes, and mine looked like a U.S. fighter plane. Dad waved me over and told me to wait for him to finish helping my brother.

I stood by Mom. She helped the girls, and Dad finished getting Peewee's kite up in the air. They laughed together when the toy, all plastic and wood, soared aloft high above them.

I scratched my legs and slapped the mosquitoes away from my ankles. I watched out for snakes in the grass. I finally gave in to my impatience and grabbed my kite from the ground next to Dad.

I didn't know what I was doing, but I'd seen it enough times on TV, and thanks to my father I'd gained confidence in my abilities to figure things out. He'd drilled into my heart over the last three months to never say *sorry*, not to end all my answers with *I guess*, and to look a man in the eye when I spoke.

I unwound the kite string, attached it to the frame and the flimsy sail, and gripped the handle. I ran as fast as I could, but the kite dragged behind me. It failed to gain more than a foot off the grass before I got tired.

After I caught my breath, I circled back and ran again, this time against the wind. I left more slack in the string as the kite rose higher into the air. My smile grew the higher the kite went. I stopped and watched the fighter plane kite grow smaller. It flew on its own and I loved it. I fantasized flying my own plane, looking down on the world, and flying so no one could catch me—not the Russian, the gunrunner, or the federal marshals. I knew I'd be safe up there, moving far and fast.

Then my kite lost control and swooped down into the only oak tree on the entire property.

"What the hell are you doing, Peté?" Dad hollered and walked toward me. My siblings' kites were aloft, and they laughed at my kite. Mom followed behind him.

I moved toward the tree and tugged at the line to free the kite. "It was an accident. I didn't mean to do it."

His face turned pink. "Are you saying 'sorry'?" My father's chest looked as if it had grown as wide as this tree. I avoided his eyes.

I yanked at the line harder; the kite lay trapped between branches. "I didn't say that."

"Stop that, useless. You're going to tear the thing apart." He leaned on his good leg. "You're going to break it, and I spent good money on that thing."

"I can do this." I wound the line back around the handle and walked around the tree to find an angle for the kite to be freed.

"Give me that thing." Dad snatched the handle away from me. "You don't have a fucking clue what you're doing."

Mom kept some distance away from us. She looked back at the other kids and hugged herself. "Eva, leave him alone."

"No. This fuck-up would've turned this thing to shit and then he'd cry about it." He moved the line erratically. Then he tried working the string like a cowboy with a lasso on TV, or like the gaucho he thought he was, and the kite broke free. It didn't glide on its way down to the earth.

I stood with fists at my side. My father set it back into the air. I watched the tall blades of grass bend with the wind and wanted a snake to jump up and bite his scarred and broken legs. It was the first time I'd wished harm on my father.

I had gotten my own kite in the air, and he had just brought me down low, as if it were his. He stood there smiling with my kite up in the air, looking like some neighborhood bully who had just stolen another kid's toy and enjoyed it.

Mom wrapped her arms around my shoulders. I shrugged them off, but she just grabbed me tighter. I didn't want to cry. I wanted to speak.

"He's an asshole."

Dad turned his head toward me, and Mom shook me gently.

I looked at his smug face. His fake nose and his mean eyes. "You're an asshole."

His eyebrows rose. "Oh, I'm an asshole?" He turned and walked toward me, kite still under his control. "Who would've bought you this kite? Another asshole?"

He handed me the kite. "Go on. Fuck up your kite."

I broke loose from my mother. "It's not my kite." I gave it back.

I left him holding it and walked back to the house. Before I closed the door behind me, I looked back and saw Mom shaking her head at Dad. He smiled and nodded his head up and down.

We ate our dinners just before sunset. As usual, Dad cooked, and we ate whatever it was he made. He sat at the head of the dining room table, and Mom sat on the opposite end. Memé sat across from me on Dad's left and Chiní between her and Mom. Peewee was beside me, closer to Mom. I sat at Dad's right hand, and though I don't recall ever being told, this seemed natural to me.

My father watched me eat and corrected me if ever I got sloppy or too quick. He wasn't big on etiquette, but he insisted on presenting me with his notion of manly dignity. If I didn't meet his expectations, he'd excuse me from the table and demand push-ups.

One night he made a vegetable stew. Like most eleven-year-old boys, I didn't want to eat a bowl of green mush in hot brown water, but I already knew the drill. It smelled and looked salty, but I ate it. Dad watched me eat slowly from the corner of his eye; the more I did what he told me to do, the less he cut me down with his words and the less I sweat. All the other kids typically ate their veggies without problems, and Memé had a strange taste for all the foods I hated. This day's meal contained one ingredient Chiní wouldn't touch: broccoli. Dad noticed.

"Eat your food, Chiní."

She looked away. "No."

Again he ordered, and again she refused. We stopped eating and watched how he'd handle Chiní's disobedience.

Chiní wasn't a defiant child. She never stole like Memé or talked back like I did. She had always followed what our parents said. Once, when our mother was strung out on heroin, she refused to eat cereal until Mom sobered up enough to grant her permission. Dad frequently praised her behavior and reminded Memé and me how we should follow her example in honoring our parents.

Chiní sat hunched over and turned away from the bowl. She spoke politely and made no eye contact. Dad lifted her chin, not too kindly. "You're not leaving this table until you finish your food." He resumed eating and so did we. Chiní continued to sit quietly and didn't pick up her spoon. Mom tried to coax her to at least try the food, but she kept her dark eyes down and her arms folded across her chest.

The rest of us finished eating and put our plates in the sink. Chiní got up to put her food in the trash, but Dad stopped her. "Did I not say you're not leaving this table until you finish your food?"

Chiní nodded and sat back down. Mom and Dad went back to their room with Peewee following. I washed the dishes, and Memé stayed with Chiní.

My sisters whispered to one another. Memé reached to grab Chiní's spoon. Chiní stopped her older sister from eating her food. She didn't want to get in trouble with Dad. Memé left her alone.

I finished my chores, and Dad came to check on Chiní's progress.

"Still?" She didn't reply. Dad's face colored red and his fists grew tight. He clipped his words. "Listen to me, Chiní. I made that food. I bought that food. I served it to you. You. Will. Consume. It." He left and I heard his door slam.

I sat beside her. She cried. She kept her sobs quiet so as not to upset our father.

Memé came back and asked me if Chiní had eaten. I said no and went back to my room to read while she stayed behind with our little sister. After a few pages, I heard Memé get up and go back to her room a few times, I thought maybe to bring toys to Chiní.

After a few chapters, I got up to check on Chiní. She was alone and had fallen asleep in her chair. Her bowl was empty, the dirty spoon lay on the table. Mom came over and picked her up. Memé walked up beside me.

Dad hollered from his room, "Did she finish?"

Mom said her bowl was empty and carried her over to the girls' bedroom.

Memé smirked after Mom had left.

The first task to refit my go-cart was to find paint. I knew the tires needed to be straightened and the steering wheel fixed, but to me it was more important to look cool.

After the mandatory morning walk, I scoured the closets for paint and paintbrushes. I found none. I asked Dad, and he considered the answer while sipping his tea. "Go seek out what you need in the barn."

I still feared the abandoned building, dark and broken like all the places children go to get killed. "I'll find another way."

"Your cowardice makes you unmanly and a genius at avoiding challenges. Makes you useless."

Mom told him to ease up on me, and he disappeared into his bedroom to pray and smoke cigars.

I gave up on finding paint or paintbrushes, but Chiní and Memé let me use their crayons. I sat on an old milk crate and decorated the go-cart with *Star Trek* icons. I wrote the USS *Enterprise* registry number, NCC-1701, on the cart's plain wooden flanks and drew crude warp engine nacelles near the wheel wells. I miss the days Crayola primary colors went far in my hands, when I felt drunk with imagination.

Dad limped outside and watched. By the afternoon I sat cross-legged in the dirt and held a *Star Trek* magazine. I wanted to copy the design of the navigation console.

Dad asked, "Want some tea?" He lit up a Marlboro cigarette. "I got the one Captain Picard drinks. Earl Grey."

I nodded. He went inside the house and came back empty-handed. "Looks like the water is out. Follow me."

I placed the crayons in the magazine like a bookmark and dusted off the dirt from my legs. "Where are we going?"

Dad cocked his head and stepped in close to me like he was going to whisper some secret to me. "You ask too much. Just obey me, okay?"

"Yes, father."

We walked toward the barn, and I felt like puking. I suspected he was going to force me to confront my fear of the place. There was nothing I could do, and he hated puking as much as crying, so I kept following. On some level I would rather have gotten murdered in the haunted barn than disappoint him. When he turned and headed toward the rear of the barn, my mouth grew dry. I had never seen what was behind the barn, and this terrified me more than the front. Still, I followed.

Behind the barn lay a field of tall grass and beyond that a wall of trees. In between stood a cluster of pipes that rose out of the ground like a patch of rusted weeds, along with a cylinder about as big as a trash can. My curiosity erased the fear. "What's that?"

Dad gestured around us. "This is your next task. Cut this grass."

"Okay, I will, but what is this?" I walked toward the cluster of metallic objects.

Dad followed me and tried to crouch, but his knees wouldn't lower him. He bent over instead, grabbed the pipes, and touched the cylinder. "This, son, is the water pump. It's not working, and I don't know how to fix it."

"Oh."

He stood up straight and stretched his back. "This grass has gotta be cut so the pump mechanic can work back here." We turned back to the house.

Dad's limp grew worse as we got closer. "I got to go to town and find the repairman. While I'm gone, I want this place mowed, do you understand?"

"I don't know how to cut grass."

Dad stopped. "What? How? I cut grass when I was younger than you and got paid." His favorite shame tactics contained condemnations along with boasts. I didn't know enough about his childhood at the time to point out that he'd grown up in suburbia with a middle-class family, while I had lived in hotels and apartments.

I shrugged. "I just don't. I've seen how you have to yank a cord to start one."

He bent over to rub his bad knee and mumbled admonishments in Spanish. He stood back up. "No, we don't have a gas-operated one. We have a regular one, like the one I used when I was a boy." He pointed to the side of the house, where a dull red push mower leaned against the wall. I had been curious about the object's purpose when we first arrived and thought it was some kind of farm tool.

"That's for grass?"

Dad smiled and clapped my shoulder. "Oh, yes, son. And you will use it. It's a good workout, and good training. Let's go."

Dad spent five minutes demonstrating how to use a reel mower.

He watched me do a patch of grass, and once he felt satisfied, he went back into the house to get his jacket.

Dad shouted from the window as he drove off, "I want a path to the pump and the area around it mowed."

"Yes, father."

"I shall return."

I waited outside for Dad. His Mercedes returned, and a white van followed him closely. It looked like the kind of van my mother had told me kidnappers used, the ones who promised candy. The side of the van had black letter decals with a name, phone number, and a quote from the Bible. Both parked in front of the house, and Dad and the other man walked out toward me.

I had mowed an area the size of my bedroom around the pump. Dad spoke to the man, a tall, lanky white man with sandy hair, but I couldn't understand what was said. We walked to the pump. The man smiled at me.

Dad took one look at my work and spit on the ground. He dismissed me with his left hand and kept his right hand in his jacket pocket. I'm certain his broken handgun was right in there.

I walked back to my go-cart and watched Dad and the man speak. The man pointed at the pump, knelt down, and rubbed the pipes, and I assumed his hand gestures showed Dad the movements of the machinery. Dad nodded and smiled. Their conversation ended when the man gave a thumbs-up and reached out to shake Dad's hand. The man's hand hung steady in the air between them as Dad fished out his right hand. Dad's movement was awkward, but the man never lost his smile. The man didn't feel bad to me, like the Russian, Dolores, or the hoarders did. To me, that meant he was a good guy.

This I also believed: Dad wouldn't shoot him, because I believed Dad was also a good guy, and good guys don't shoot each other. Besides, my father's gun couldn't shoot.

When their hands finally met, I stopped watching them and returned to my work on the cart.

I continued painting the console until Dad came over.

He pointed to the door with his chin. "Let's go inside. Let the man over there do his work."

"Okay." I gathered the magazine and crayons and went to my room. Dad followed me.

"When I was a boy, I made and sold go-carts to the kids in my neighborhood."

"I know. You already told me."

His whole body nodded. "Yass, yass. I did tell you that." He grew quiet and sat on the corner of the bed Peewee and I shared. "Listen, don't flush the toilet until he finishes repairing the pump. Tell your brother and sisters too."

"Okay." I opened the drawers where I kept my meager wardrobe and placed the magazine next to my underwear. Dad had made me fold them into small squares and insisted that every night I hand-wash the pair I'd worn that day.

"I'm going to tell your mother. I'll be in the living room." He put most of his weight on the least damaged leg and made for the door. He stopped just outside. "Hey, I love you, kid."

"I love you too, Dad."

The repairman knocked on the door just before sundown. I had been in my room playing with Peewee. I got up and my brother followed right behind me.

Dad opened the door and invited the man inside. The man spoke while wiping his hands with a blue rag streaked with oil and grease. "Well, Mr. Cuesta, I replaced the pump solenoid, and it should be working right well now." The smile never left his face.

"Who's that?" Peewee asked, and I didn't know if he meant the repairman or Mr. Cuesta. I shushed him and listened to my father speak. Mom and my sisters had filed in and watched from the couch.

"That's great, David." He walked over to the sink, and after a few sputters, water flowed again in our house. "Ah, thank you, David. And thank God." The English name of Allah sounded strange in Dad's mouth. At the mention of God, David's smile grew even wider.

"Well, Mr. Cuesta, I know you're new in town and you have a lovely family. It'd be my honor if you'd come over to our house for Thanksgiving this week. Family homestead is only a few miles up the road from here."

I'd forgotten that Thursday was Thanksgiving, had forgotten the holiday entirely. Dad had lectured us that it was a white supremacist holiday, that it celebrated lying and cheating the native peoples of this continent, who I thought were almost all extinct. He'd said it was at best an excuse to sell shit to fat, wealthy Americans.

"Ah, that's very kind of you, David." Dad looked around the living room. "But we have plans already."

David pocketed the rag. "Of course. Well, have a happy Thanksgiving and have a blessed night." He held out his hand, and this time there was no hesitation from my father.

Dad walked him to the door, and after the bolt was snapped in place he turned and rolled his eyes.

Now that the show was over, my siblings melted back into our parents' room, and I sat alone in my place at the dining table. "Dad, why did you say no to his invitation?"

He stopped midway to the kitchen and came over to sit beside me. He leaned in close. "What do you mean?"

I couldn't keep up with his eyes. They were the color of the sea, and to me even deeper. I lowered my eyes and pretended to look at something on my hands. "He seemed nice. I thought maybe we should have Thanksgiving over there." In the span of time between the invitation and this conversation, I had already envisioned a friendship with his children and playing games with our go-carts.

"Fuck Thanksgiving bullshit, but let me tell you about people like him." Dad placed his hand over mine. His complexion differed, his pink and mine olive. "They are polite, and they love to spout all this nonsense about Jesus Christ and God, but deep down they aren't to be trusted."

I had no experience with people like David, humans with frank kindness and earnestness, but I believed that people outside of the family are only kind when they want something. I'd learned that from the strangers my mother used to invite over to party while Dad sat in prison.

He continued, "Cruel men speak of God and scripture excessively. Don't listen to their words; pay attention to their actions." He ran his hand over my hair. "You're a good soul, Peté, and I love that about you."

He left me at the table and went back to the kitchen to boil water for tea. "Still want some Earl Grey?"

I said yes. This man my father described was much like himself. He endlessly quoted Qur'anic verse and praised Allah, but his actions were otherwise profane. My instincts had told me David was good, and so was my father, but I didn't know what to believe anymore.

Like every other place we'd stayed since we'd been running from the feds over the last three months, the time to abandon Gainesville finally arrived. I had not been prepared and didn't know the reason why, but I wasn't surprised when Dad woke me up one early morning in December. He only told me to pack my shit and help my brother.

Peewee had a dull look on his plump face, his smile gone and replaced by thin lips and furrowed brow. He no longer wore diapers. Dad had made sure he'd finally gotten potty-trained, and he looked older now. He jumped off the bed we shared and held his toys loosely in his hands. His chubby legs stomped while he moved back and forth from our drawer to a plastic bag.

I felt the same way he looked. This house in the middle of nowhere had become a home to us, our first real home ever, with a present mother and really present father. My siblings and I had grown close as brothers and sisters here. I don't know when, but even the rivalry between Memé and I had disappeared; we played together, laughed with each other instead of at each other, and shared secrets.

I grabbed a toy. Peewee's current favorite was a *Star Trek* Ferengi action figure. "Hey, Peewee." He looked up from the suitcase and plastic bags. I flew the figure around the room and made the whoosh noises from *Star Trek*, supplemented by the special effects of engine hums and phaser noises.

Peewee smiled. He grabbed another toy, and we flew around and around each other in our room, in our home, one more time.

9

Our car pulled into a shopping plaza so Mom and Dad could buy cigarettes and coffee. Like all the other roadside malls we had seen in rural Florida, it contained a big-name grocery, beauty salon, liquor store, maybe half a dozen boutiques, and a drugstore. This pattern of development had been consistent. The only differences were the names on the signs, and I collected these names to help me pass the time.

My father turned off the engine and I peeked around him from the backseat to see if I recognized the names of the stores. I recognized most of them, but there was a new one I hadn't seen before, and I knew what it sold. I bounced in my seat. "It's a bookstore!"

My parents turned around from the front seat. Dad's eyes were bloodshot from driving six hours. "Calm down, Peté."

Mom held my baby brother on her lap. She wiped the sweat from his brow and adjusted the seatbelt that held them both. She tried to rouse him from his road nap. "Wake up, Peewee."

My excitement infected Chiní beside me. She wanted to go inside too and, if nothing else, just get out of the car. Memé sat behind Mom and seemed completely uninterested in the store.

Dad shut both his eyes like a double wink. That was how he said *I love you* or *let's go*, depending on whether he was high or not. I opened the door and jumped outside with Chiní close behind me. There was a little chill in an otherwise bright central Florida afternoon. I held Chiní with one hand and shoved the other deep into my pocket to keep warm.

We'd been on the move for a while. We'd stay a few days in a motel or a family friend's apartment just long enough for Dad to make some money. Our destination was always the next temporary place. I never knew where we were going, only where we had been, and Dad let me track this on a map like a navigator. He didn't tell me why we traveled like this, but I knew it was to keep the federal marshals guessing as to his whereabouts. It was important to me they didn't catch us, because if they did my family would be broken apart.

Our current location was a small town in Alachua County, between Gainesville and Orlando. Parked around us were older model pickup trucks and station wagons, so our white 1991 Mercedes-Benz 300 stood out. We were hardly inconspicuous in this part of Florida anyway. Our names were clearly not English, and Chiní did not look white. Dad instructed us to say, if anyone asked, that we were tourists from Miami visiting Disneyworld, and of course his name was Joe Cuesta, not Evaristo Calderón.

I stood outside shivering and waiting for Dad to get out. He opened the driver's door and I heard Mom say, "His dimples are showing." She opened her door and got out of the car with sleeping Peewee and Memé right behind. They went to the Publix next to the bookstore. I held Chiní's hand and saw that her dimples were showing too.

Dad took a long time to stand. "Go on inside, I'll be there in a second."

Chiní and I opened the door, and she ran off to look at the coloring books by the register. The scent of the paper intoxicated me. It smelled like freedom to me. The rows of neatly shelved books were brighter than the sun outside. People inside held books and smiled. Hardcover, mass market, and trade paperback stories all in front of me. I'd never seen so many books in one place before, not even in my school's library.

I hadn't been to school in five months. I'd never finished a novel before. I wanted very badly to read.

I smelled Dad before I saw him behind me: cocoa butter and cigars. "Go ahead and look around. Don't get comfortable."

I immediately went to the main display of fiction. There were some author names I recognized from movies and TV shows: Stephen King, John Grisham, and Danielle Steele. None of their books seemed interesting to me, so I moved deeper into the store.

I passed through the romance section in the store without stopping. All the images of shirtless men holding women embarrassed me. There was a military-themed shelf, but the men on the cover looked like the ones who burst into our home on that summer night. I stopped to look at the religious and philosophy books full of wisdom and explanations, and I liked their cover art.

In the back of the store, I found the science fiction books. Out of the dozens of titles, one grabbed my attention: it was a *Star Trek: The Next Generation* book called *Vendetta: The Giant Novel*, by Peter David. I didn't know of the novel and had never heard of the author, but I fell in love with the cover. It had my favorite characters, Captain Picard and Guinan, and my favorite bad guys, the Borg, with the majestic USS *Enterprise* rendered above the title. I had to have it, and I believed my father would get it for me.

The time I had spent on the lam with my father had so far been difficult for both of us. Before this odyssey, I had never spent more than an hour with him, the maximum allowed during prison visits. He took it as his duty to whip me into shape, but my fantasies and lack of manly attributes at eleven disappointed him. His first arrest had come early in his life, then he became a father at sixteen, a cocaine millionaire by eighteen, and had lost it all up his nose or from seizure by the feds before I'd been born; I did not compare to him, and he liked to remind me of this.

I clutched the novel to my chest and ran over to him. Dad was at the front looking at coloring books with Chiní. I presented the novel to him, asking, "Dad, can I have this?"

He took the novel from my hand. Dad examined it front and back. He returned it to me. "I can't afford this. Put it back." The price on the cover was $4.95.

My vision blurred, and my sinuses started to betray my emotions, the kind he didn't tolerate. "But Dad, why not?"

Dad ignored me and put the coloring book Chiní held back in the rack.

"But Dad . . ."

He turned to me. His eyes were exactly like the ones I saw in the mirror every morning, but his were meaner. "Put that back. That's an order."

I imagined everyone in the store watched this. I obeyed him to avoid further shame, and it was the right thing to do to keep a low profile.

And then the bookstore no longer smelled wonderful. The colors of the books dulled. I felt everybody's stare and put the novel back in its spot. I said good-bye to the adventure I'd never experience and returned to my father.

Dad stood and I could tell from the way he leaned on his good leg he was disappointed to see me in such a state. He patted my sister on the shoulder and said, "Let's go get food, Chiní." She smiled and reached for my hand. He only pointed to me. "Go to the car. I'm going to use the bathroom."

I stepped out of the bookstore. Mom had returned to the car and played with Peewee while smoking her Marlboro Reds. The windows were rolled down, and I could hear my brother's laugh every time she blew smoke through her nose. Memé was eating a deli sandwich. She leaned out the back and smiled.

I opened the door for Chiní and helped her climb into the backseat. She sat between me and Memé, a buffer and neutral zone between us.

Memé knew something had happened and asked Chiní, "Is he going to cry?"

Chiní stopped smiling and looked at me. "Are you?"

"No." I hid my face from her and refused the food Mom handed to me. I counted the number of trucks in the plaza to get my emotions under control. There were only three different colors: white, black, and gray.

Another game I played while we evaded the cops was noting the differences between us and the people along the journey. In this town, like most places in between hideouts, school buses carried kids. Men of all kinds went to work. Women ran errands and their kids wore baseball jerseys.

The differences told me everything. I used to go to school. Mom let Dad handle everything. His job was selling drugs.

Dad limped out of the bookstore. He opened the car door and turned so that he could put his good leg in first and rest his weight on the driver's seat. He sighed and leaned forward. Dad pulled something from his waistband, where he usually carried his hand-gun. He threw the novel at me. "There. I want you to read it, front to back, and report back. Do you understand?"

"Why does he get something?" Memé stomped.

Dad said, "Because he'll read it."

I held the cover and ran my fingers over the letters. "You said you couldn't buy it."

The car turned over and the engine purred. "That's true. I didn't buy it."

I knew what he had meant. "But Dad, isn't stealing bad?"

Mom said, "Peté, don't be ungrateful. Eva, you could have been caught. What would have happened if you'd been caught?"

Dad put his black Ray-Bans on and took a cigarette from her pack. "Well, then, we better move out." He backed out of the parking space without looking at his mirrors.

I gave the book to Chiní so she could touch its letters too. I asked him again. "Dad, isn't stealing bad?"

The car moved faster, and even though I couldn't see his smile, I could hear it when he revved the engine. Wind rushed into the car. Once he'd merged into the flow of traffic, he sipped the coffee Mom had bought and answered. "Yes. It is a sin."

Chiní gave me back the book. I said, "Then why did you do it?"

He blew out smoke and merged onto the interstate. He yelled so I could hear him over the wind. "Well, son, because you're worth it." I saw the smile on his face in the mirror. It wasn't happiness; it had the look of mischief, like Memé, and he wore it every time he outsmarted the feds. He enjoyed the crime.

"Thank you." The back of his head was slick because he like to put cocoa butter on his hair to keep it healthy.

Dad shook off the affection. "I meant it. I want a book report in a week."

"Okay." I opened to the first page and started the adventure that was offered to me, stolen for me.

I finished the book in less than a week, but Dad never asked for the book report, and I never asked him for anything again. I knew he would risk everything for the thrill.

A few hours later, my parents told us we were again heading toward my grandmother's apartment. Dad said he had to go on a trip to New York and that it was best if Memé and I stayed behind so they could spend more time with the younger ones, Peewee and Chiní.

Memé had cried about fairness, but Dad suffered none of it. She sat quietly next to me with her arms crossed while tears seeped from her green eyes. Mom had tried to console her from the front seat, but she refused to speak. I, on the other hand, would be very happy to see my grandparents, and the little ones were looking forward to getting some attention from Dad. No one spoke further about it until we stopped around Fort Lauderdale.

Dad pulled into a shopping mall. He said we were here to buy winter clothes only for those traveling north and nothing else. Memé glared at him like she was plotting his murder.

I took in the surroundings. People hunted for parking while some walked back and forth to their cars, many with bags of stuff, and everyone wore grim smiles on their faces. Behind all this commerce, a Toys R Us dominated the mall.

When we'd left Louisiana to go on the run with my father, Mom had kept us from bringing any toys. I didn't have too many anyway, but not because I was too old to play with action figures. We were poor. I mostly played with my friends' toys.

Christmas was everywhere, but it was still a few weeks away. I already knew my father wouldn't tolerate anything about gifts or trees. He'd made himself perfectly clear during one of our long car ride conversations.

He'd said, "Christian bullshit. They stole it from the pagans. No one knows when the great prophet and the messiah Jesus was born, except Allah. It's idolatry." He'd spit a wad of phlegm as big as a hummingbird out the window. "Capitalists, money worshipers, fooling fools into spending money they don't really have."

I had asked, "Pagans worshiped idols, so Christmas is still pagan then?"

Dad had laughed and winked at me in the rearview mirror. "Yes, son, it clearly still is." Memé had stuck her tongue out and called me a kiss ass.

Before heading into the mall, I grabbed my *Star Trek* novel and prepared to endure the raw boredom in a store with nothing I could buy.

It was a warm and sunny December day. Dad led us to a Burdines. He wore his Ray-Bans and a fedora. On the walk he ignored Mom's comments and our questions. Normally he never kept quiet and always answered, but this time he was very quiet. He guided us with grunts and hand signals. Once through the door, a wall of cold air hit me, and my father breathed out a sigh and immediately set to shopping around with Mom and the other kids. I stood nearby and followed them around racks of clothes and read my book while they were in dressing rooms. My head hurt after a while because of the expensive perfumes that reminded me of Dolores.

Dad kept stopping to look around at people. He behaved like a prey animal in a wildlife documentary, constantly checking to see if a predator lurked nearby. In those shows the cameras always knew the animals were in fact being hunted, and they never aired one that didn't have a life-or-death scene. I think I was old enough to know that nobody would watch those shows if it were any other way. I wondered if there was a camera watching me and if it panned over to the predator just out of my sight.

The federal marshals didn't appear, but Dad never let down his guard. We left, with me and Dad carrying the shopping bags full of winter clothes for my parents and the little ones. We stopped just before the crosswalk, and he turned back toward Toys R Us. Peewee cheered and the girls instantly thanked Dad. I kept quiet just in case this was one of his tests.

As soon as we stepped inside the doors to the toy store, he grabbed the bags of clothing I'd been carrying, and he looked at each of us. "Pick out one thing." He shifted the bags to one hand and raised a finger at each of us. "One thing! Make sure it's something we can carry around."

My sisters ran straight to the doll section, kept segregated from the other toys. Those aisles radiated pink. I grabbed Peewee's hand, and we skipped and laughed to the action figures. There, tucked between G.I. Joes, Transformers, and Batman, was the *Star Trek* section.

They had Captain Picard in his uniform as well as a variant in his casual coat from the famous Darmok at Tanagra episode. Data, Worf, and the famed engineer Geordi La Forge too. LeVar Burton's character was my favorite at the time because he acted just like himself on the *Reading Rainbow* show. It also seemed that he was the most important character, because everyone, even the daring Riker, relied on him to find a solution for all the ship's problems. I wanted to grow up to be an engineer like him so I could fix anything too.

Peewee immediately picked out a generic Ferengi figure. After watching some episodes with us, Dad playfully called my little brother a Ferengi because he had really big ears, much like the prosthetic ones the fictional aliens wore. My brother loved the nickname, and it was a fun joke between them.

I told Peewee the toy was a good choice, and he pointed out some other characters I might want too, so we could play together, but I didn't want any action figures. The starship USS *Enterprise-D* sat on the top shelf of the aisle.

The toy had special effects sounds and light-up warp engines, and best of all it had already been painted. All I had to do to fully assemble it was plug in the nacelles, place stickers at the appropriate spots, and slap in four AA batteries. Peewee oohed and aahed and smiled his toothy grin.

The only problem with getting Dad to buy it was the size. About as long as my forearm and awkwardly proportioned, it certainly would be difficult to pack. I remembered he'd told me once that if you don't ask, you don't get. Tall as I was, I easily reached the toy without any help and went to the checkout line where Mom stood. Dad waited outside smoking.

My sisters took a little longer choosing their toys, but once we'd all had our pick Dad returned. He tucked the Marlboro Reds in his back pocket and examined each of our selections. I prepared my arguments and had a list in my head of why I deserved this: I'd lost weight, learned how to cook, helped take care of my baby brother, and cut acres of grass with a push mower.

When Dad looked at my USS *Enterprise-D*, he didn't say a word. He pointed at the cashier with his chin and all the toys ended up on the checkout counter. Dad paid with a crisp hundred-dollar bill.

We left the mall with the trunk full of new toys and clothes. My *Enterprise* toy didn't fit, so I held it on my lap until we arrived at the hotel. The family spent the night watching TV from the two twin beds, while I put together the *Enterprise*. I sat on the rollaway bed a few feet away from them. There wasn't much to assembling the toy and it even came with the AA batteries, but the memory of my last project and the brutal critique of my skills from Dad had me double-checking where stickers went and how the warp nacelles connected to the secondary hull.

Later that night, Dad rolled a joint with Mom. I held out my finished project. "How does it look?"

He looked up and licked the paper to seal the joint. He passed it to my mother and crossed the short distance to sit on my bed. "Show me what you did."

I pointed out the placement of the stickers: the ship's registry, name, and logos of Starfleet aligned and placed in their correct places.

"Okay, good. See what you can do if your mind is disciplined?" He clapped my shoulder and kissed my forehead.

I held my toy. The novel my father had stolen for me sat nearby, its book spine already broken and the pages dog-eared from reading on the road. I knew an episode of *Star Trek* aired later that night. I had all these *Trek* things, but none of my friends ever liked the show. I'm pretty sure Peewee liked it because I liked it. "Dad, I'm curious about something."

He placed his arm around my shoulders and smiled. "That is such a shock. I thought I knew my son." Mom passed him the lit joint. "What's your question, Peté?"

"Why do I like *Star Trek* so much?" My eleven-year-old mind had never questioned its obsessions. I simply accepted what I liked but had never put much thought into it until then. I had liked sports for the glory of winning, and video games had been fantastic tests of puzzle solving and reflexes, but nothing else had captured my mind.

Dad took a hit and passed back to Mom. He turned his head away from me and blew out the smoke. The white cloud rose from his lips to the hotel's popcorn ceiling and dispersed. The only thing thicker than the smoke was the smell. He turned back to me and smiled. "Because Allah wills it so, my son."

I didn't like the answer. It was the same as if he'd said, *I don't know, son. Who cares?*

Then he stood. "You'll grow out of it." He went back over with Mom to the twin bed and watched TV with the rest.

I placed the *Enterprise* toy on the writing desk near me. I balanced the ship on the box it had come in so that it wouldn't fall or place too much stress on the neck that connected with the saucer section. I picked up my book and read a scene with Guinan and Picard discussing the concept of vengeance and acceptance.

I know now why I like *Star Trek* so much. The knowledge came with age and, more importantly, some perspective. The first episode I ever watched happened after a fistfight. I was eight years old, and the fight was important to me because it was the first fight I hadn't lost. Put it another way: I didn't get my ass totally kicked. I had knocked out the other boy, an older and bigger kid than me, and had stood victorious over him while he cried for his mother. The neighborhood kids had rooted for me, because this other boy was a bully, and they went wild when my fist had connected with his face. I stood over him, high on the chemicals my body had produced for me to fight.

Then his parents drove up and ran out of their car toward us. The kids took off running, and I did too.

I had told Mom what had happened, and I felt guilty because I'd liked hurting him. Moreover, I could've hurt him really bad, and then I'd be in trouble and my family too. My mother had acted indifferent to my anxieties and told me to sit still. She had smiled and applied hydrogen peroxide to the cuts on my knuckles and cheeks. I think she was proud of me.

I had winced and complained about the sting, so she'd turned on the TV for a distraction. *Star Trek: The Next Generation* had played.

I cannot remember the episode, but it showed that hunger and poverty had been eliminated with hard work, ingenuity, and science. In the future of *Star Trek*, violence among humankind had disappeared, and the people had united for the common goal of exploring the universe and bettering themselves.

After that episode, I watched anything *Star Trek*. Whenever my stomach felt empty because the food stamps weren't enough, or Mom hadn't paid the electricity bill, or my knuckles bled, *Star Trek* gave me hope for better days.

My father was wrong. I never outgrew *Star Trek*.

Dad had dropped Memé and me at my grandparents' apartment in South Beach and left for New York with Mom, Chiní, and Peewee. It seemed hard for me to believe that Mom had brought us here three months earlier, at the beginning of our fugitive life.

I spent the first few days reading while Memé sulked, but she cheered up when our grandmother took us to the family *Noche Buena* party. My aunt had hosted one every Christmas I could remember.

Being at the gathering felt like being on another planet. I'd been living apart and in a different world, with my father. He had been explaining to me how things weren't as they appeared, but my extended family preferred to project appearances. I've often wondered over the years how they could speak to me at our gatherings as if we were one big happy and healthy family and yet fail to see my mother's obvious drug problem and our desperate childhood. Dad believed in ugly truths; they believed in pretty lies.

As soon as we arrived at the party, my aunt and cousins asked questions about Mom and our little siblings. My father had once told me my grandparents were master liars, and I witnessed that night how right he was. They deflected all inquiries and, when pressed, made up a plausible story. We got some presents that night and went home with full bellies.

Mom and Dad returned just after New Year's, 1993. We met them outside the apartment building on the corner of the street. Our grandparents didn't go outside with us; they'd told us to go downstairs with our things as if we'd just finished a weekend sleepover.

Dad had parked a few feet from the building entrance and stood on the curb. The Mercedes had been replaced by a white Chrysler LeBaron. He still wore Ray-Bans and a fedora with a band made from owl feathers. He smoked a cigarette while Mom and my little siblings sat in the car and played behind the rolled-up windows with the A/C on.

Memé ran and hugged Dad for a long time. He gently pushed her head back and kissed her head. "We can't stay out in the open too long." She kissed him back and jumped in the new car.

Dad and I regarded each other. He looked like a Panama Jack model. I couldn't keep my eyes on his, so I compared the lopsided soles of his New Balance sneakers to my Payless sneakers. I'd looked forward to being with him and yet felt dread. I knew my performance would be graded, and I feared he'd think me insufficient.

His eyes focused on my chest and stomach. "Looks like you didn't get too fat." He tossed his Marlboro into the gutter and waved me closer. We embraced.

"Did you do push-ups?"

"No."

"Alhamdulillah, my son is not a liar." He squeezed me tighter. "Did you read?"

"Yes."

"From the Qur'an?"

"Sometimes."

He let me go. "I love you. Get in the car."

The new car was smaller than the Mercedes. Memé sat in between Chiní and me, and we had to move our asses around to find the seatbelt buckles. Peewee sat on our lap and exchanged hugs with us, and Chiní reached her hand over to squeeze my shoulder. We'd only been apart a couple of weeks, but Chiní and Peewee seemed to me to have grown over the holidays. We drove away, happy to be reunited.

We checked in to a motel that night, somewhere in Broward County in one of the smaller cities that orbited Fort Lauderdale. The room was clean and had cable TV.

We left the next morning just before checkout time and drove all day. Dad wouldn't say where we were going, and he'd lost the map I'd used to help him navigate. The pine trees reminded me of the area near the house in Gainesville, but we weren't far from palms either. That night we stayed in another motel, and it wasn't as clean as the one before.

For weeks we drove to gas station pay phones and slept in whatever place took cash and had a vacancy. We never spent more than two nights at one place and never returned to the same motel or hotel. We'd go as far as north and west as Alachua County and drive up and down from Miami to West Palm Beach.

After we'd check in and get settled into a new room, Dad would grab a black duffel bag I'd never seen before his trip to New York, and he'd disappear for a few hours. It stressed my mother out and she'd pass the time smoking a joint and sleeping, while I kept my head in a book or watched TV with my siblings. Each time he left, Dad said, "I shall return," and each time he did, sometimes with more cash in his pocket and a big smile.

Mom and Dad kept us fed and content by buying fast food, the kind that came with small plastic toys and wasn't halal, and allowing us to watch movies late at night. Dad had continued to demand ten push-ups from me, and I did them more out of habit than obedience.

I kept reading. I had started to write down some of the adventures in my head, mostly in the form of comic strips. Before long, life on the road started to seem normal to me.

Even after all these years I never found out why Dad kept us on the road for weeks after he returned from New York. I'd trusted he simply couldn't find a safe place for us to remain while he made the money toward getting our family to Argentina. Perhaps my father shifted bed-down locations often to throw off the marshals, but in my memory it seemed more like wanderlust than strategy.

My parents fought more often. Dad cursed more than usual, and Mom talked back to him with greater disrespect than I'd ever heard from her before. One afternoon my father pulled off the road after Mom had yelled at him to take a break and let her drive. He'd been behind the wheel all night and morning, our destination still unknown to me.

"Get out," Mom said once Dad stopped the car. We were parked on the long grass alongside a one-lane asphalt road scarred with cracks. Tall pines flanked the route as far as my eyes could see.

"Listen." When my father got pissed, "listen" was a one-word sentence.

Mom didn't give him a chance to continue. "You need to listen to me. You've been driving too long. You're not thinking straight."

Dad flung his door open. He used the steering wheel and gripped the car roof to climb out of his seat. "Fuck you."

Mom got out and slammed her door. "Fuck you, Eva."

"Suck my dick," he yelled as they passed each other at the trunk of the car.

"I already did," she retorted.

We watched this argument and my siblings kept silent, until I laughed at the dick-sucking comment. Then Memé laughed, and the little ones joined.

Dad climbed in as slowly as he'd gotten out and started to laugh with us. "Your mom is funny, isn't she?"

Mom said nothing and turned off the radio. Dad slept and she drove.

When Mom got sober, we spoke about these times. She told me that during those weeks on the road she'd gotten sick of my father's craziness and that his hypocrisy had reached a level she could no longer suffer in silence. She told me that early in our fugitive life, my father had confessed to her that he'd had sex with one of her friends, Hannah, after she'd sheltered him during Hurricane Andrew after his escape.

Dad had explained to my mother that he hadn't had sex in years and just couldn't help himself. Besides, Hannah found him irresistible (how my father had the balls to say this, I do not know). Mom told me she was no saint and had had plenty of her own indiscretions during the years of my father's incarceration, so she forgave him and even gave her friend a nickname: Hurricane Hannah.

However, my mother hadn't accepted my father's excuse for infidelity while they were together. He'd confessed to my mother about another one of his infidelities during their trip to New York. During our stay at Bleau Fontaine, on a rare occasion Mom had taken us out shopping, my father had remained alone with Dolores. He claimed she'd made advances on him, and he'd felt he had no choice but to comply. "After all," he'd said to my Mom, "we were staying at her place rent free. The least I could do was eat her pussy. But hey, at least I didn't fuck her."

I don't understand why he told my mother this. Maybe he felt guilt, or this was part of his bizarre sense of honor. Mom never spoke to Dolores again and never forgot my father's bullshit reasons.

Eventually the road exhausted my family. The highways turned to county roads, then to city streets, and back again. I didn't know how money worked, but I knew that Dad was bleeding cash because we got fewer treats as the days progressed. Some days one or more of us kids would get dropped off with my grandparents, and this helped relieve the stress on my father and save money.

We were now into February 1993. My siblings had just been dropped off, and I spent the afternoon talking with Dad about philosophy while my mother drove. I had stopped asking where we were heading weeks ago. The radio stayed off and Mom and Dad chain-smoked from the same cigarette.

We talked about a question that had been growing in my head. I'd just heard of Aristotle from an episode of *Star Trek* and was curious, so I asked the most knowledgeable person I knew about him and the great philosophers of the Mediterranean.

Dad insisted on steering the conversation to Islam, and he expounded all the ways the Greek philosophies had been saved from the fires of ignorance of the West. "Some philosophers," he said before taking a deep drag from his cigarette and passing it back to Mom, "may have been prophets from Allah."

I held my breath and waited for the open window to carry out the smoke. "How many prophets have there been?" I never liked the stink of cigarettes, but I loved the scent of his cigars.

"Many thousands; not all are known. Every nation has had at least one. But there are five you must know." He counted off on his fingers. "Adam, the first man. Abraham, who followed the covenant with Allah and will be the commander of all nations on the chosen day. Moses, who delivered the Jews from slavery and the

Ten Commandments. Jesus, who is the messiah for the children of Israel. And the last one on this earth, Mohammad, peace be upon him and his descendants." Mom passed the Marlboro back to him, and he smoked it down to the filter.

I'd known these names but not that there were thousands of prophets lost to history. The sky turned the color of bruises. This close to the city, there was too much light pollution to see stars. "Are there prophets on other planets? Like for aliens?"

He tossed the filter out the window and rolled it up. "Only Allah knows."

"But what do you think?"

"I believe that if there is life, and Allah created all life, then he would guide them with a prophet and messenger. If he wills it." He turned toward the backseat and looked right into my eyes. "Do you know who your imam is?"

My father had told me that, in Shia Islam, Imam Ali, cousin to the Prophet, and his lineage are the true heirs of the caliphate, not in the militaristic sense of the word *caliphate* but as the leader of all Muslims in the absence of the messiah Jesus and all the other holy men returned for the end times. There were thirteen imams after the death of the Prophet, including his cousin, and they were all believed to be infallible. The last imam was taken from earth and was biding his time in Heaven with Jesus, not dead.

He squeezed my arm. "This is important. Your imam is Mohammad Ibn Hasan Al-Mahdi. Repeat it, son."

I obeyed.

"When you die, you will be asked, and if you can't answer that then you are lost to me." His eyes were wet with tears, but he didn't cry, and the rest of his face was impassive like the philosopher statues I'd seen on TV.

He made me repeat the name five more times, and then he was satisfied. He turned around and settled into a nap and ended our conversation on philosophy and history. I stared at the dark world passing outside and wondered what the end times would look like on another planet for other peoples.

On the road I'd seen places I couldn't have imagined existed. There were roadside restaurants and motels that looked like they were from a scary movie. Their names were strange and sometimes even funny, like one we came across that had a Chinese restaurant named the Fu King across the street from the Horne Hotel. Dad had marveled at the brilliance of the owners. "This is great. You stay at the horny hotel and go to the fucking restaurant after. Outstanding!"

There were places where no people lived, vast tracts of land that seemed to me as wild as early America—abandoned homes and lonely graveyards so old the stones were smooth and covered with vines. My parents drove through towns that only had one store, one school, and one traffic light or none at all. Some had signs, but I didn't recognize the names from geography class in school, and some of them didn't even show up on our AAA travel-sized map.

I fantasized about what life would be like in places like this, to be apart from the city and the world, and to live with only our family and very few friends. I decided it was idyllic and maybe that's how we'd live in Argentina. I was sure there were places like this over there, and I made a note to myself to ask Dad for a map of Argentina so I could find their small towns that had no names along roads.

It was past nine at night by the time Mom pulled into the parking lot of a motel along a county road somewhere west of West Palm Beach. There were no cars parked here, only big rigs. I don't remember the motel's name, but I do remember the sign said "Vacancy" in bright red neon lights and a sign below advertising "hourly rates available." Next to it was a pizza restaurant named Pizza.

My mother patted Dad's shoulder and he blinked at her, then opened the door. He looked at me. "What did General MacArthur say as he quit the battlefield in the Philippines?"

"'I shall return,'" I replied.

He smiled. "I shall return," and he got out. He adjusted the money belt he'd been wearing lately and walked to the motel's front office. Mom lit a cigarette, and I unfolded the map to see where we were, but she couldn't find this place on it.

My father returned with a pizza and told Mom to pull up closer to our room. We stepped out of the LeBaron and I stretched my stiff leg muscles. The parking lot smelled like diesel and grease. The tractor-trailers hid the view of the street from me. Dad opened the door to the room, and Mom grabbed a duffel bag from the trunk. I grabbed my backpack with a change of clothes and a new *Star Trek* novel Dad had bought me, not stolen that time, at our last city stop.

The room smelled like cigarette smoke and bleach. Everything here seemed shabby and cheap. The corners of the furniture peeled like rotted leaves, and the carpet felt stiff and had dark stains. Next to the king-size bed was a machine that took coins just like the rides outside of grocery stores, the kind for little kids to ride lacquered horses and rocket ships. The strangest thing was that the ceiling had mirrors.

Dad went to the bathroom and Mom put the pizza box on the table. "Go ahead and eat, *gordo*."

The cheese pizza vastly improved the smell of the place, though it tasted cheap and probably wasn't halal. I realized then that haram food must be cheap, and Dad had once told me Americans did this on purpose to make life difficult for Muslims and Jews.

I ate only two slices, because I knew more than that would anger my father. Mom said, "Go ahead and have one more. We won't be stopping for breakfast tomorrow."

After I finished, I opened my backpack to settle into my novel. Dad stumbled out of the bathroom with a smirk and heavy eyelids.

I looked to the ceiling and saw my family upside down. "Dad, why are there mirrors up there?"

A stupid smile grew on his face. He shrugged. "So, you can better watch your woman ride your dick." He giggled. "Or so she can watch you thrust into her."

My face grew hot, and I kept my eyes on the book.

Dad said, "Come over here, Peté." He stood by the table and stared hard at the pizza like he thought he'd recognized something in the cheese and grease.

It would be pointless to tell him Mom gave me permission to eat a third slice, so I put my book down and got ready for my ass to get chewed. Instead of calling me out for being fat and overindulging on haram food, he grabbed me by the shoulders and hugged me.

"I love you, son." He pulled away and squeezed my neck.

His face was all bliss, more carefree than I'd seen him since we'd left our home in Gainesville. "Are you okay?"

He laughed and said nothing, only gazed at me.

Mom shook her head. "He's high. Very high."

Dad walked over to her and hugged her.

She patted his back and rubbed him as he smiled and cooed. "Let's go to sleep now."

Dad took off everything but his underwear and lay down on his side, humming a tune to a song I didn't know.

I changed into shorts and a T-shirt. Mom changed into a nightgown in the bathroom and turned off the lights. I slept between them and stared into the dark mirrors.

10

We left the hourly motel and went to my grandparents' to pick up my siblings. Dad drove us to the Russian guy's house where we'd stayed months ago. After I unloaded the car completely of our things, it made me think we'd be staying put for a few days—until Mom said we'd leave as soon as Dad came back from an errand.

I got very worried that something bad was going to happen. The longer we ran, the more unlikely it seemed we'd continue to survive. I told him to stay.

Dad turned at the door. "I shall return."

I spent the night miserable and a nervous wreck. My anxiety spread to my brother and sisters, but Mom consoled them with food and eventually they went to sleep. For the first time I could remember, I felt no hunger. Mom gave up on me and dealt with her worry by popping pills. She slept until morning.

I kept away from my siblings and sat on the couch alone with one lamp on. I ran scenarios in my head of the ways this night could turn out, and none of them ended with our success. It reminded me of an evaluation in *Star Trek* that all cadets had to complete in Starfleet Academy: the Kobayashi Maru, a no-win scenario that is supposed to teach someone how to handle failure.

Next day the sun rose, and Dad returned. His mood shone bright; he came in whistling with a new duffel bag. I threw my arms around him, and he squeezed me right back. He sat me down and I prayed thanks to Allah, just like he'd taught me. The morning had brought a miracle, and after hours of dread, I felt wonderful and giddy.

The other kids were still asleep. Mom walked out of her room and Dad opened the bag and handed her a couple of pill bottles; the dark containers glowed the same color as orange juice. They went into their room, and I slept a few hours on the couch.

We left the Russian's house the following afternoon.

We spent nights at nice hotels again, with rooms that were billed by the week and often had the word "resort" appended to their names. We ate good food, swam in pools, and watched cable TV.

I'd forget at times that we were hunted fugitives and how one slip-up could end all our dreams of escape to Argentina. Dad kept me from getting complacent by enforcing long walks and on-demand push-ups. He kept a strict eye on my diet, but I didn't mind it anymore.

It was April, and spring had come. Every day shone bright, the air felt warmer, and the places we traveled pulsed full of life. The people we met were friendly, and I enjoyed laughing with perfect strangers. Our current hideout was a beachfront motel near Fort Lauderdale. A swimming pool sat right outside our door, but the white sands and ocean sang to me every night. I had grown to love the smell of sea air and the taste of dried saltwater on my lips.

Late that night, I had fallen asleep on the room's sofa while I'd been reading. When I awoke the next morning, Mom and the other kids had already left to swim in the pool and Dad had stayed behind while I slept. When I opened my eyes, he was writing in his little black book and drinking coffee. He was dressed in a white T-shirt and shorts that didn't quite cover the scars on his knees.

As time moved on from his escape, my father had grown melancholic. He was constantly in pain and spent lonely hours flipping through the little black book. Each day he'd write in it and leave the room to make a call. After an hour or two he'd return, and each time he stood a little smaller. I'd noticed money had gotten tight again.

Dad put the little black book away and said, "Good morning, sunshine." It felt like both an endearment and a reproach. He didn't mind if I stayed up reading, but he still wanted me to be an early riser. He tossed my clothes over to me. "Let's go for a walk on the beach."

I no longer appeared like a chubby kid with tits. All the forced walks and push-ups he'd prescribed had made me stronger, and instead of an unrestricted diet of microwaved food and high-sugar cereal, he'd made sure as often as possible that I ate small portions of good food. I had energy now and naturally woke up early on most days. I got dressed, and we both walked out barefoot. I waved to Mom and the kids on the way to the sea.

He took his T-shirt off, and I did the same. We walked in silence along the back shore of the beach. People tanned and played in the sand all around us.

"Dad, I have a question."

As long as I had known him, he valued honesty above all and answered any question I had to the best of his ability. He expected me to reciprocate, even if it was something I shouldn't have known. It had always been the basis of our relationship. "I have answers. Maybe you'll understand them."

"What was your father like?"

He didn't say *hum* or *ah*, like he usually did before answering me. My father kept his eyes straight and out to the horizon. The wind and waves gently played against the surf. Birds squawked and tourists laughed—the symphony of the coast.

Just when I thought I'd finally found a question he wouldn't answer, he laughed. "My father was a judge."

"Like a lawyer?" I wasn't sure if he meant his dad was judgmental or that was his profession. Dad nodded his head slowly. I think back now and believe he meant both.

He didn't elaborate more on the topic. We took our time walking, and the crowd of people thinned. I picked up seashells for Mom and the girls and searched for shark teeth to give my brother.

I wanted to know more about his father, because I thought I might learn more about me. "Did he have a gavel and wear robes? Or is it different in Argentina?"

Dad put his arm around my shoulder and pulled me close to him. I was almost his height. "Something like it, but different. My father was a poor judge."

"Oh, he was bad at it?"

Dad laughed and his smile turned down, like he had bitten a lemon. "No. No. He was very good at being a judge and in the profession of lawyers."

"Your family was poor then?" Dad had never seemed poor to me.

He kissed my head. "No, we were not poor. 'Poor judge' meant he was an honest judge. He didn't take bribes. He was an honorable man."

There on his lips grew a smile. His eyes stayed closed for a second too long. I asked, "You didn't want to be a judge like him when you grew up?"

He barked a laugh. "Most of my brothers became lawyers. One of my sisters. Not me!"

He let me go and limped. I slowed down to his pace. Dad said, "He died when I was very young, only fifteen, and I took care of him because after the fifth stroke he couldn't even wipe his own ass. He was old, and I was the seventh child of seven kids."

"How old was he when he died?"

"He was fifty-five. Not old really, but he'd had a lot of strokes and the seventh one killed him." He clapped my back and chuckled.

I laughed just to laugh with him. "That doesn't seem old to me. Why did he have so many strokes?"

Dad took a deep breath. "He worked a lot, and being an honorable judge took a toll. And it runs in the family."

I thought about this and what it'd mean for my future.

Dad picked up the pace again and hummed a tune. I continued to push and dig about his father. "What was he like?"

Dad squirmed and scratched his belly. He'd never hesitated with me; he'd told me all manner of raw truths before without blinking: Mom's addiction to sex, consequences of drugs for the body, his love of the criminal life, but his father haunted him like nothing else.

Dad spit a massive wad of mucus on the sand. "He was very strict. I'll tell you a story. When I was young, about your age, I went to prison for the first time."

I found it hard to believe a judge would allow his eleven-year-old son to go to prison, but then an honorable man wouldn't use his position to show favor. "Why?"

"I was very much like you. I built things, liked racing cars made out of wood, and dreamed of driving them." He stopped for a moment and looked at me. He shook his head, and we continued to walk. "One day a friend of mine asked me if I could accompany him to run an errand for his dad, who was out of town."

He moved our path closer to the water, and the tide washed our feet. "His dad ran a bar with prostitutes, what's called a brothel. Anyway, all we had to do was show up and collect the money from the guy running the bar. We didn't know the police would show up too."

"The cops put kids in jail?"

"Sure they do, even here. But Argentina is different than here." My father had a great deal of contempt for the United States. Most of it was tied to our history that's steeped with hypocrisies: African chattel slavery, broken treaties with exterminated Native peoples, and interventionist wars. But the one thing my father liked about

America was the prison system; the treatment of prisoners here was far better than in all the places he had been locked up.

"They put you in juvie?"

"Oh, no. We were in there with the prostitutes and everyone else they'd roped in. At least they kept us with the whores instead of the men." He smiled. "The whores were nice to us boys. They comforted us. And of course, the whores loved me."

I rolled my eyes. "How long were you in jail?"

He stopped smiling. "Not too long. My father came eventually. He was a judge after all, and he was known by the cops. He was embarrassed. He used his position to get his son out of jail." He scratched his nose and ran his fingers along his goatee.

"Was he mad?"

Dad said, "Furious, but serious. He never yelled."

The tide rose, so we moved farther up from the shore. Dad continued, "My father told me, 'Son, this is the last time I bail you out of jail,' and true to his word he never did it again."

"What about your friend? Did he get him out too?"

He nodded. "Yes. And he got the whores out too when I told him they took care of us. I'm telling you, the whores loved me."

I wanted him to stop mentioning the prostitutes and tell me more about his father. "What happened after? At home?"

Dad grew silent again. We had been walking for at least half an hour. Behind me the hotel looked like a small concrete block. Ahead of us the hotels got bigger.

He stopped and our gazes locked. "Before he died, before he was crippled by a stroke, he told me, 'Son, you're either going to be a faggot or a criminal. Please be a criminal.'" I looked away and we continued the walk.

I still had many questions. Even now I still have so many things I want my dad to unpack from that statement. It was a keyhole to his soul and character and, I believed, a confession.

In that moment I should've asked why his father had said that, or if he was gay, or if he forgave his father. Instead, I asked, "Dad, why is everyone around us naked?"

Dad snapped to attention and we both stopped. All around us lay men and women with no clothes. They lay on beach towels tanning their wrinkled skin and flabby flesh. Old men's penises hid under bushes of gray hair. The women's breasts and bellies were pink from the sun.

Dad said, "Oh. This is a nude beach."

I felt my face growing hot, hotter than the sun, and looked away to my father's feet and to his scars. "Shouldn't we go?"

He lifted me by the chin and smiled. "Are you afraid of nakedness?"

I shrugged and put my eyes back down to the white sand.

Dad said, "Look at that man's dick."

I peeked. I could barely see it, but it looked like mine except uglier.

Dad put his arm around me. "See, son, that is normal. Don't let anyone tell you different."

"I know."

Dad continued, "All those big dicks you'll see in porn have been sucked and fucked unnaturally. Healthy ones look like Michelangelo's David. Remember when I showed you that statue?"

"Can we go home now?" I was still a boy, uninterested in girls, and embarrassed by the naked body.

He kissed my forehead. "Okay, it's fine."

We turned around and walked away from the naked people. We asked no more questions of each other the entire way back.

A couple of days later, my parents told us they needed to go on an errand. They instructed us to stay put until they returned, though I had no idea what else we could do. Before he left, my father said, "I shall return."

Peewee and I played with our *Star Trek* action figures on the floor of the hotel room. My sisters watched music videos and sang along. There was a knock at the door.

Memé and I looked at each other. It wasn't the secret knocking pattern Dad had taught us, so we shrugged and ignored it. Probably the housekeeping, I thought. The next knock came heavy and rattled the checkout sign that hung on the door. Memé turned off the TV and huddled with our little siblings on the bed. I got the door.

Two men stood outside. They wore neatly pressed slacks and had clean haircuts and no facial hair. I knew they were cops before one of them flashed his badge. "Federal marshals. Is this the Evaristo Calderón family?"

For the last nine months Dad had trained me for this question. I didn't need to think about it. "My father's name is Joe Cuesta."

The one with the badge smirked. "Yes, we know. That's one of his aliases. Let us inside, kid." He didn't make eye contact with me and tried to see behind me like I was an inconvenience. The agent behind him sighed and turned away and scratched the back of his neck. He seemed more human to me.

I tried to close the door, but the lead agent pushed right on through. I ran back to the bed where my siblings held one another. The feds were followed by regular cops with uniforms and weapons. They must've been stacked by the door in preparation to breach, kind of like they'd done in Baton Rouge.

The more human fed said, "We have your father and mother in custody. Where are your father's things?"

"My father's name is Joe Cuesta."

He kept asking me other questions about Dad, and I kept telling him they'd made a mistake and that wasn't my father.

I couldn't believe they'd captured Dad. He was too smart for that. Any minute these lawmen would leave having found nothing, and then Dad would sneak in, and we'd run again.

Chiní and Peewee buried their crying faces in Memé's chest. Memé didn't cry. She held the little ones and kept asking me, "What do we do, Peté?"

"Say nothing. Our father is Joe Cuesta."

Dad had trained me well. I didn't cry and, like he'd told me, I wouldn't give up the ship. The cops tore through our room, probably looking for evidence.

The meaner fed joined in the questioning. Then Memé joined the little ones in sobbing. I continued to hold out.

I don't remember their interrogation. I retreated into myself and recited in silence all the aphorisms Dad had taught me about stoicism and toughness and how Allah would look after us.

Law enforcement had been closing in. They'd watched as my family lived as fugitives and waited for the best time to apprehend my father.

When I turned sixteen, my father sent me a bunch of different legal documents to read. He wanted me to summarize their contents, and I thought he wanted to test my ability to comprehend law. I now believe he wanted to see if I, like most of his family, had the knack for the legal profession. I passed his test, but I told my father I didn't want to be a lawyer and had already formed an unfavorable opinion of lawyers. Of this he approved.

In the collection of affidavits and motions for the court he sent me was the arrest report from our fugitive days, filed by the marshals two days after his arrest. This is what the agents recorded:

"On May 19, 1993, deputies proceeded to area of Hacienda Inn at 1924 N. Atlantic Blvd. Ft. Lauderdale, Florida, based on information received by this office. A white Chrysler LeBaron with a Florida tag of DED 89D was parked in front of the inn. At about 9:30 am a woman, later identified as Maria Calderon, was observed entering the driver's door. A male who was identified as the fugitive entered the passenger door. The Chrysler left the inn parking lot and headed south bound direction on Ocean Blvd. After making a turn onto Sunrise Blvd and heading west, Deputies and Ft. Lauderdale police arrested Calderon at the Nation Bank at Sunrise and Seventeenth Ave.

"Calderon was read his Miranda Rights by Deputy McDermott after he began to make statements. After being read his rights Calderon said he wanted to talk to the deputies. Calderon said that Maria Calderon had only done what he had ordered her to do in assisting him in his escape and his fugitive lifestyle. Calderon was asked if he had any contraband or weapons in his room at the Hacienda Inn. He said he had a pistol in the room but he had not bought it. Calderon said someone had given him the gun. Deputy Smemo obtained the exact location of the pistol and returned to the Hacienda Inn. A Colt Commander .45 caliber pistol, serial number 70SC51714, was recovered in a closet. Also hypodermic needles were also found. Deputy Smemo remained at the Hacienda Inn until Calderon's mother-in-law came to the scene to take custody of the four children Calderon had left unattended in the hotel room. Calderon had in his possession at the time of his arrest identification in the name of Jose Ramon Cuesta.

"Maria Calderon was arrested by the Ft. Lauderdale police for auto theft. Calderon was transported to the Federal Courthouse to appear before the duty magistrate on the escape warrant.

"While being transported to the Federal Courthouse Calderon asked what he was being charged with. He was informed that a warrant for escape had been issued in the Middle District of Louisiana. Calderon stated he had not escaped but had just walked away."

I don't know how much time had passed at the Hacienda Inn. I stayed locked away in my head until I heard my grandmother's voice.

The cops left the room. Alle told me it was true; Dad had been captured. Then I wept in her arms.

Years later, I learned from my mother what had happened behind the scenes.

A week before the feds raided our Baton Rouge apartment, another visitor had arrived. Mom had gotten a call from an old associate of my father, someone she hadn't heard from in a long time. She had us clean up the apartment and dress in fresh clean clothes. Usually she didn't care about our appearance, not when family came over or when random men showed up at her doorstep. She was evasive when I had asked who was so important that we had to work so hard.

Mom turned off the TV when she heard the knock. I had been following the 1992 Summer Olympics and had enjoyed seeing Team USA's basketball dream team sweep the competition. She seemed frantic and touched her clothes and the pictures on the wall. After one more knock, she had us stand up while she opened the door.

A stranger stood with his hands behind his back and a big smile on his face. He was a balding Black man with black-rimmed glasses. He greeted us like my father did: "As-salamu-aliakum."

We replied in chorus in the same manner we spoke to our Dad: "Wa-aliakum-salam."

Mom waved her arm like a hostess at a restaurant guided a dinner guest. The stranger entered. She turned to us, saying, "Kids, this is Chuck. He is a friend of your father."

Chuck appeared no older than my father. "Thank you for inviting me, Lele. You have beautiful children and a lovely little home." He had a strange accent, not Latino or Haitian, and his speech pattern didn't sound like any part of the United States I'd seen on TV.

It wasn't unusual to receive a visit from one of Dad's friends or associates from the narco-trafficking world, but I'd never heard of

Chuck before. Mom rubbed her hands a lot and giggled when he looked at her.

Chuck asked each of us our names. He spoke softly and his words came across as gentle. He saw the plastic McDonald's Olympic basketball team collector's cup Mom had bought me and asked which one was my favorite player.

I waited for my mother's nod. "Michael Jordan."

Chuck smiled. His eyes were intense. "I must admit I grew up in Chicago, so that makes me a Bulls fan too."

I enjoyed gaining his attention and rattled off Jordan's stats from the last game I had watched.

"You're a smart boy, just like your father." I laughed. I didn't know what to say, so I looked at the carpet so he wouldn't see me blushing.

Chuck turned to my sisters. "Such lovely young ladies. Truly Frankie is blessed by Allah." He used my father's nickname, the Anglo shortening of Francisco. My kid brother stood behind Mom and waved at Chuck. "Ah, and this is his newest blessing. Hi, little boy!"

Mom kept the door open. "Okay, kids, go outside and play while we talk." We knew the drill. Anytime a man showed up at our door, we were expected to disappear. But not this time.

Chuck said, "No, Lele. I cannot stay." He slightly bowed from the hip. "Tomorrow, I will bring my wife and daughter over for dinner if you'll have us."

Mom put on a smile and gave a nervous chuckle. She wrapped her arms around herself. "Yes, that will be fine."

He backed away to the door. "Seven?"

Mom hummed her approval, and Chuck said, "See you all then. As-salamu-aliakum." He turned and walked outside.

Chuck arrived exactly at seven, and we had dinner with his family. His daughter was Peewee's age, and his wife looked younger than Mom. I don't remember the details, but he was the politest man I'd ever known to be associated with my father.

Chuck was the reason Mom had needed to talk to Dad alone on that last Sunday prison visit in Baton Rouge.

The reason we had moved to Baton Rouge turned out to be because my father had started to provide the federal government with information. He had bargained what he knew of drug cartel operations in exchange for a nicer facility where we could visit him more often. It had proved to be a dangerous gambit.

Chuck was a killer. He had worked with my mom and dad back before they'd had me. He'd been sent by Dad's former associates to deliver a message: we know where your family lives. Dad had escaped prison as a response to the immediate danger to us. I never saw or heard of Chuck again.

My father had been caught in a dilemma of his own making: trust the feds to protect his family or run. Contrary to the popular idea of a prison, the one my father had escaped from had very little to keep him imprisoned. The place was a medical facility first and a minimum security prison second; it had no high fences and nobody at the gates to prevent my father from simply walking out and getting in the car of an associate he'd called for a getaway. Hurricane Andrew then provided an opportunity to escape down to Miami. No cops would be trying to apprehend him during a Category 5 storm, and somehow he didn't get killed in the process.

Mom had also told me he would have attempted to break out even if there had been no hurricane. In merely attempting escape, he'd communicated to Chuck and his associates he wasn't going to snitch anymore.

In any case, Dad did what he had always done: take charge of his own fate regardless of the consequences to others.

The federal marshals explained to Alle what was going to happen to Mom, and they allowed Alle to take custody of me and my siblings. My grandmother drove us to her apartment in Miami Beach. Every few minutes she would say, "*Ay, Dios mío.*" I took turns crying with my sister the entire trip.

We'd left behind many of our possessions and had taken only what could be carried in trash bags. The rest was taken by the feds. I abandoned my books but kept the USS *Enterprise* toy Dad had bought me.

It had grown dark by the time we arrived. Abo stood at the door to greet us with Hershey's chocolate bars. He'd arranged blankets and pillows on the floor. We ate the treats at their small table and sobbed ourselves to sleep.

Alle posted bail for Mom, and the cops released her the next day. Months later, the feds decided not to press charges against her for aiding an escaped federal convict. I knew the real reason was because Dad had cut some deal with them, because he'd always said he'd do that for her.

She walked into my grandparents' apartment wearing the same clothes I'd last seen her in. Abo didn't hug her at the door. We rushed to our mother, and she embraced us all in her arms. Her hair was knotted, and her knuckles had dried blood. She stank like piss on cold concrete.

My grandparents left us and retreated to their room.

Mom looked at each of us and said she loved us very much. She had the shakes, and I'd already learned from my father those were symptoms of heroin withdrawal. Then Memé pulled from her trash bag a pill bottle and handed it to Mom. The label had the word *codeine* spelled out, and I had also learned from Dad it was an opioid. Memé had stolen it from under the feds' noses, along with enough money for Alle to bail her out. Mom popped two into her mouth and swallowed them without any water.

We made the bed on the floor for her while she showered. Memé and I tucked her in. Mom sobbed and cried, the kind of deep, guttural crying that comes from pain, and then the pills hit. Her breathing slowed. Her children slept around her, and just as before, so many months ago in Baton Rouge, I slept at her feet.

We ended up that night much like how we'd started out as fugitives but in some ways much worse.

11

Summer arrived, and my twelfth birthday came and went. Mom had a court date the next day to meet her public defender.

Tears stained my pillow every night the first month after my parents' arrest, and then one day they stopped. A numbness had set in. Besides, real men don't cry, and my father wanted me to be a man. I hadn't heard from him since May, and Mom didn't know where the feds had taken him.

We remained with my grandparents in Miami Beach for so long that we'd de facto moved in. There was nowhere else to go. Somehow two elderly adults, one strung-out addict, and four kids managed to get by in a 740-square foot, two-bedroom, one-bath apartment.

Alle and Abo didn't look directly at Mom, and they'd stopped speaking to each other. My siblings and I spent the first few weeks simply eating and sleeping. The recapture of Dad hadn't had as big an impact on Chiní and Peewee, but I could tell it still hurt them because they had become more silent.

My aunt took Chiní and Peewee out on the weekends, but not me or Memé; I believed she left us alone because we were so traumatized that we were hard to look at, like terminal patients in hospice.

Memé and I spent our days indoors and watched a lot of TV but not together. Without our father, we had fallen back into our old relationship habits. We fought and tore each other down daily. I didn't pray or read the Qur'an. I got fat again. We were back on food stamps, and I ate and ate and ate. I knew this would disappoint my father and dishonor all the work he'd put into teaching me how to be better, but eating made me feel good and I did anything to avoid feeling pain. He'd taught me avoiding pain was a sin, yet he took heroin to manage his.

My mother handled her pain by disappearing during the night. I roamed along Ocean Drive and looked for her in bars and clubs. When I'd find her, she'd be either dancing by herself or drinking Long Island iced teas with a random shit-faced guy.

School started the following August. My mother had kept herself together long enough to spend a day enrolling Memé, Chiní, and me at Fienberg-Fisher Elementary School; Peewee was still too young for pre-K.

Fienberg-Fisher went from kindergarten to sixth grade, and I thought it unusual to have a middle school grade in an elementary school. Since we hadn't completed our grade levels the year before in Baton Rouge, we all started right where we left off. I had to re-enroll in sixth grade.

We walked to school every morning without my mother, from Eighth Street to Fourteenth Street on Washington Avenue. Our grandparents were too old to walk and too poor to drive. Memé and Chiní held hands; I kept mine in my pockets. I listened to the rumble of bus engines and our cheap Payless shoes hitting the pavement. Miami Beach had started to change. Bums slept at the bus stops now, and more bars and night clubs had opened. Strippers and tattoo parlors conducted business within three blocks of the school. The morning sea air had been replaced with the stink of last night's beer and piss. If the city was a living thing, it had a hangover.

We arrived early to eat free breakfast. I spent the time before the first bell doodling and writing. I'd continued to write my own comic strips. I'd taken a liking to the ones I read from the English edition of the *Miami Herald* my grandparents tossed away in the corner of their bedroom. My favorites were *The Far Side*, *Calvin and Hobbes*, and *Marmaduke*. They were light and funny, and at the same time insightful, and I thought one day I'd like to make something similar.

The sixth-grade kids at Fienberg-Fisher were nicer to me than the ones I had briefly been with in Baton Rouge. No one asked any questions about where I had come from or made fun of me for any reason. All the kids were either Hispanic or Jewish, or both, and I blended in with my Cuban background.

The justice system finished charging Dad for escaping prison and possessing a firearm and added more years to his sentence. He then got transferred back to Homestead Correctional Institution, near Miami, the last place he'd been before the transfer to Baton Rouge. As soon as he was granted visitation rights, we traveled by bus and train to see him.

New guards had started working since the last time we'd visited, but they remained mean-faced. The toys in the waiting room were still dirty and incomplete. We stood in line while the adults were searched for contraband. Finally, over two hours after leaving Miami Beach, we were allowed into the visiting area.

My father again wore a prison jumpsuit a size too big, and with the same number stenciled on the back: 39941-019. His face looked swollen, and he moved much slower than the last time we were together.

Dad said, "As-salamu-aliakum."

We huddled around him, and he embraced us. He moved us to an open table, and we sat. He asked questions and we answered. When it came to me, he wanted to know if I had been reading the Qur'an, walking, and treating my family with respect. I kept to honesty, and while the answers hadn't satisfied him, he kept a smile on his face while I spoke about starting school again. Mom interrupted a few times by bursting into tears. She buried her face in his shoulder and stained his jumpsuit with snot and mascara. At the end of the hour, the guards called all the inmates to stand against the wall. Dad stood with them and waved us good-bye. The prisoners watched visitors leave and waited to be searched for contraband.

I enjoyed the return to school. The teachers cared about my ideas and encouraged me to participate in class. A progress report came home with me in October, and the grades were high. Alle cooked flan as a reward. My mother partied too much to notice.

When a due date arrived to turn in a science project proposal, I submitted the magnetic transportation idea I had talked to my father about when we'd been hiding out at Dolores's place. My teacher wore an astonished look while I explained to her the concept of using magnets to propel a car. I told her I'd use an electric current to generate a magnetic field on a wire and then have a magnet latched on a toy car. I was only twelve and a bit fuzzy on the details of maglev trains, but she didn't interrupt me for any details and only smiled back when I asked if that could be my project. The other kids in the class called me a nerd, but it lacked venom and we still played together at recess.

The school principal called Mom in December. He wanted to schedule a conference with her about my academic progress. She actually showed up.

The afternoon after the meeting, she sat beside me while I did my homework on the tiny dinner table at my grandparents' apartment and told me what had been decided. "You're going to the seventh grade in January."

I stopped writing. "What?" I'd been preparing my science project, writing the research topic and hypothesis.

She snorted like she had a runny nose and coughed. She was sick a lot lately. "The principal said you were too advanced for sixth grade. Your teachers think you should go on to seventh."

"But I don't want to."

She smiled at me. "You're a smart boy. Besides, aren't you supposed to be in the seventh grade already, right? Weren't you in sixth grade in Baton Rouge?"

I shrugged. I'd long ago grown used to having no control over where I went, but at that moment my feelings changed. Her vacant stare and apathy planted the seed of resentment.

She played with my hair. "You're so smart, Peté." She left to go smoke weed on the living room floor.

I quit doing my homework and left the apartment. Mom never asked where I went.

I opened the door to the emergency stairwell and sat on the landing. The building was full of the old and disabled, so I never saw anyone climb up or down from my perch on the eleventh floor. I'd started hanging out there in the summer to avoid people, and I enjoyed the space because I could sit there alone with my thoughts and dreams.

In January 1994, I went to Nautilus Middle School. I left behind a few friends at Fienberg-Fisher and missed the relative comfort of still being in an elementary school. The middle school was so far away from my grandparents' apartment I had to take a school bus again.

I stopped doing well in class and my grades tanked. The kids were meaner and the teachers totally disinterested. Alle tried to encourage me with food and occasional five-dollar bills, but she eventually gave up and I was on my own.

My grandparents kicked us out in February. Their neighbors complained about all the noise we made, and the administrative offices reminded Alle that the building was not meant to house a family with four children.

Mom had gotten a job and used the money to put us in a motel room. She worked at a hot dog cart in downtown Miami. She got compensated like a waiter, which amounted to a couple dollars an hour plus tips, and only worked a few hours a day. She lasted there until she realized she couldn't afford her habits by selling junk food to men in suits.

After that she found work at a dry cleaner, which were plentiful in Miami Beach. She folded and pressed clothes all day, at minimum wage and under the table. A pattern began to appear: every month or two she would go on an extended bender, lose her job, and find another dry cleaner.

We had the bare essentials to survive and relied on school for meals, but her addiction cost more than our grocery list. A fact I had learned: food stamps go for 50 percent of face value on the street.

We moved often, from motel to motel all along Miami Beach. These places were worse than the worst hideout spots we'd been at with my father. I had a checklist for crummy motels: cockroach infestations, lice, fist-sized drywall holes, drug dealers, stained carpets, and broken bathtubs.

On one occasion during a long summer, Mom got fired and couldn't find another job fast enough to make rent. For a few weeks we slept on the couch and floor at the home of one of her girlfriends in Hialeah. Her nickname was Pepina, which means cucumber in Spanish. I'd never heard of her before, and she didn't know my dad. She had mood swings and slapped around her kids—an illiterate twelve-year-old son and an eleven-year-old daughter with a scar on her face. I didn't get along with them, and Pepina scared me. I kept my distance and spent the days playing video games on her son's Super Nintendo or walking around the neighborhood.

Mom overdosed at Pepina's and then after running out on the hospital bill, found another dry cleaner job and moved us back into a motel in Miami Beach.

Eventually, my mother divorced Dad. It was a simple affair because they were never legally married, only wed in Islam. I'd never known before their split that they weren't really husband and wife, though it did explain why she had her second husband's last name on her driver's license and not Dad's. They recited the Islamic verses to part ways and that was all.

Mom explained years later that Dad would never do a civil marriage because he'd been a wanted fugitive as long as she'd known him and never wanted to show up in a courthouse for a marriage certificate.

Mom hooked up with a guy named Bernardo shortly after the divorce. My father gave him a nickname: Bastardo. Unlike the other men Mom had met, he didn't just leave after having his fun. He moved in with us and took an interest in her and her children's well-being. He played with my younger siblings and bought trinkets and sweets for us. I refused to accept that Mom could find happiness without my father. I disliked him only because he wasn't my father, and I did everything I could to make their relationship fail.

I talked back to Bernardo, called him many terrible names, some my father suggested, and disrespected the support he provided me and my family. This man never fought back, never harmed any of us, and was patient with me. In other words, I was an insufferable little shit.

Bernardo didn't use anything more serious than weed. He didn't like how much Mom depended on opioids and antidepressants. He tried, but her addiction wouldn't be domesticated. Eventually Bernardo got fed up and left her. Ever since and even now I've regretted playing a part in destroying their relationship. Bernardo made my mom happy, and he desired nothing more than to have a family.

Mom couldn't make rent without Bernardo. We moved back in with my grandparents one more time.

—

In the midst of all the family drama, drugs, and demons, I finally took my father's advice and took religion seriously. I wanted to become the kind of man he respected, a goal I yearned to achieve more than anything.

I adhered to the five pillars of faith. I read the Qur'an and prayed five times a day. I fasted during Ramadan and devoured books on Islamic laws, histories, and traditions. These activities calmed me and provided a sense of purpose and, more importantly, a connection with Dad.

We'd speak over the phone and exchange letters about theology. I'd have questions prepared, and he'd always have answers. My father sent me more books he'd ordered through the prison library from prominent imams.

But the more I read, the more uncomfortable I felt about what modern Islamic scholars preached.

After finishing a passage that encouraged the reader to spurn non-Muslim friends and require the conversion of spouses before marriage, I quit the book. The scholar's arguments about piety and purity by way of isolation from the other made no sense to me and didn't fit with the concepts of the religion, a religion of peace and tolerance, as I understood. His writings sounded like hate and prejudice.

Most of my friends were Jewish, my best friend was Wiccan, and all the girls I liked were Christian, but the imam argued they were at best a distraction and at worst did the work of Shaytan, the devil. My father needed to explain, so I waited until the second Saturday of the month, when he had enough minutes saved up from working in the prison library.

The phone rang and I sat in the living room of the apartment we'd had with Bernardo. Once the Islamic greetings were exchanged, I got straight to the point. "Dad, I don't know about this imam. I think he's wrong."

He laughed at me. "Who the fuck do you think you are to question someone so learned? Ignorant, that's who you are." The phone connection from prison sometimes made his voice tinny, and the insults sounded far away.

"But Dad, are non-Muslims really bad?"

"Listen, son. You need to live a halal life, and the best way to do this is to be among Muslims. There is a Muslim community in Argentina I want to join once we're there. In the meantime, like I've told you so many times, find a mosque in Miami and pray there."

I still wasn't persuaded. Dad went on and on about what I needed to do and how to do it and not be a coward. I paced around the couch and shook my head at everything he said. Finally, I couldn't keep quiet. "Dad, you have friends that aren't Muslim."

"Yes, I know, but . . ."

"And the other books I have here say that drugs are haram. The Qur'an explicitly says their effects are haram, but you do drugs and get high. I also read that a good Muslim must abide by the laws of his host country, so long as they don't directly interfere with Islamic practice. Nothing here in the USA prevents you from being a good Muslim, but you break the laws." I didn't add on that the books I'd read had been ordered and delivered by the U.S. Postal Service.

He sighed. "My sins are my problems with Allah. And I accept my judgment."

I waved my hands around. "So it's okay to do drugs but not okay to have a Jewish friend or love a Christian girl?"

A stern voice on his end in the background said something, but I didn't understand the words. He cleared his throat. "I want you to become the best you can be, to live as a real Muslim . . ."

"I don't want some man from the other side of the world to tell me how to live my life." The words fell out of my mouth. I wasn't even aware of what I had said, only that it felt right. Being angry felt natural, though I couldn't say why. I kept on going. "This educated man doesn't even know anything about science or the world." From somewhere in my memory, I recalled one of the Islamic books I'd read, about a council of imams a century ago that had convened a series of meetings to determine if photography was haram. If they were so learned, why were they so ignorant of the world?

I blurted out, "This imam is a fool!"

He hummed and spoke slowly, "He is more knowledgeable than you, Peté."

His condescension wouldn't push me off my soapbox. "No, all he does is tell Muslims what to do."

Dad raised his voice to drown out the commotion behind him. "Knowing Islam is all you need."

"Apparently, doing what I'm told is all I need." My mouth was on autopilot. "I don't think there's anything wrong with having friends and people in your life who aren't Muslims."

A man yelled on my father's line. Dad said, "Listen, I have to go. Pray and all will be made clear in time."

He rushed through his Islamic parting phrase and hung up after I garbled the reply. I had no idea what was going on over there in the jailhouse.

After that call, I stopped reading the Muslim clerics' books he'd sent. I still read the Qur'an but stopped praying regularly. The more I lived, the more people I loved and hated, the less I believed anyone had true answers. It's hard to quit religion overnight, so it took years for me to finally let go of the faith. His religion was not for me. I didn't want to be the person my father or these scholars believed I should be.

Dad of course never approved of my decision to leave the faith. Apostasy, he'd told me, is punishable by death under some interpretations of Islamic law. I reminded him so was drug trafficking. I grew bored with his admonitions and annoyed with his Arabic greetings and stopped speaking to him about religion.

Years later I deployed to war in the Islamic world and saw with my own eyes how Muslims lived. My father had always put them on a pedestal, as if they were somehow better than other people merely for believing the Prophet's message, but that was his delusion. They were no different than I, or anyone else. They did drugs and drank alcohol, had tattoos, whored, killed, lied, and loved. They were just humans trying to survive in shitty situations, just like me.

I do believe in a higher power, but I'm not convinced anyone on this planet has any knowledge of that being's nature or how to live in accordance with its wishes.

Without my doing any work, middle school had graduated me to the eighth grade and then on to Miami Beach Senior High. I had started to develop anxiety and depression. I continued to eat my emotions, and then when food ran out, I sneaked out and walked the streets for miles at night. I navigated by neon lights and watched the city party its ass off. As long as I moved, I felt all right.

In school I joined band for a creative outlet and learned to play the flute. I liked the sound of the instrument; it felt like being nimble and free. Music gave me something to focus on other than my troubles.

Music education cost money, but I never paid. There were programs and fundraisers for poor families to still have a way for their children to participate, but I hated taking advantage. I didn't feel shame for being poor, mostly because I knew we could have afforded it if Mom didn't spend so much on drugs.

I kept apart from the other band kids. I didn't want them to know me. I played for a while, then quit and sat out the competitions and trips, then returned later just to play again.

The school news advertised a chess club, and I joined that during my absences from band. I'd only ever played against Dad, and we'd stopped playing as our relationship deteriorated over the disagreements about faith. The teacher who ran the club taught openings, midgame strategies, and endgame puzzles. He took us to competitions, and as a team we performed well. I wasn't a particularly good player but not the worst either; I usually finished the tournaments with two wins, a draw, and two losses.

I enjoyed being in the club, and the teens in it were my kind of misfits. We were socially awkward and escaped our lives by using our minds. When we got bored with chess, they taught me a card game called Magic: The Gathering. On the weekends I joined them in a role-playing game called Dungeons and Dragons; my favorite character class to play was a rogue, and I think it was because of my father. We talked about science fiction and fantasy books, argued over the feasibility of the theoretical technology on *Star Trek*, *Star Wars*, and *Babylon 5*, and spent hours at school discussing the lore in *Lord of the Rings*.

Dad didn't approve of these distractions, other than chess, and cautioned me that these activities were haram and unhealthy.

Dad once called out to me as I headed on my way out the door to meet up with my friends. "Peté, these friends of yours are idiots."

I said, "Yes, but they're my idiots." He laughed at me and said he loved me even if I was useless. I still have these friends.

Home life kept getting worse and worse. Mom got sicker and sicker, and Abo had been diagnosed with Alzheimer's. Caring for him was difficult, especially since no one took care of themselves. I felt lost.

I ceased going to my father for guidance. Every prison visit and every letter I received had the same type of advice. *Pray, Peté. Read the Qur'an. These concerns of yours are nothing, and all you need is faith in Allah. This will give you the strength and courage to face your fears and achieve your goals. Stop playing these fantasy games with your idiots.*

When he got tired of hearing about how I felt, he'd said he had no desire to hear my problems because he had his own. "Real problems, unlike yours," he'd said, using his favored terms for me—"useless" and "unhappy." His problems were with other convicts, federal attorneys, corrections officers, and occasional stays in solitary confinement.

Dad encouraged me to research the GED and take it as soon as possible and leave school. He told me school taught un-Islamic ideals and was a waste of my time and talents. He still wanted me to become an agricultural engineer and be ready for the disaster he believed would occur on May 5, 2000. The goal was to be in Argentina, reunited and prepared, before that day.

I had stopped listening to my teachers and cared nothing for their grades and assignments. They only put me down, and some told me I was a delinquent and a burden on society. I don't blame them; they couldn't help me and had no way of figuring out how to help.

I continued to go through bouts of depression, drop out of school in the spring, and show up again next summer hoping for a fresh start and some food.

At fifteen, I wanted to leave home. There wasn't any reason to stay, and I wasn't the first to figure that out. Memé had dropped out of seventh grade and left to stay with Dolores.

The motels didn't feel safe, and I hated seeing my mother strung out, slowly killing herself. Besides, my father reminded me constantly I was a burden, and I didn't want to make life harder on anyone, especially my poor grandmother, who took care of us and Abo; his Alzheimer's had progressed, and he'd started to forget her.

I needed to get a job.

I thought I'd apply to a fast food restaurant or grocery store because I could get paid and eat for free. My plan was to save enough to get first, last, and security deposit for my own apartment. I'd send extra money to Alle to help support Chiní and Peewee. I didn't know shit about how fifteen-year-olds could possibly have their names on rental agreements and utility bills.

I knew I needed to get some documents together and work on a résumé. I waited for a day when Mom was in a good mood but not too high. I asked for my Social Security card to get started.

She sat on her bed and smoked a joint while listening to a Jimi Hendrix best hits CD Bernardo had bought. She took a big hit and spoke after exhaling all the smoke. "You don't have one, *gordo*."

"How come?" I knew all my siblings had one. She needed them for food stamps and other government assistance.

"Well, you're not a U.S. citizen."

I was born in Aruba. Mom had told me before that after she got pregnant the first time by Dad, he'd wanted to start his life over again in Argentina. She said he wanted to make a legitimate life to raise me. They'd traveled to Buenos Aires and reached out to his family. They'd begun to reconnect and heal old wounds, and his cousin helped him get a job as a car salesman.

They lived like this for a few months. I asked Dad later why this chance to turn his life around had failed. He explained that the Argentinian military had control of the government and right-wing death squads had made people disappear. Any Argentines with a criminal record were fair game.

Mom was eight months pregnant when Dad had told her they had to leave Argentina. He went back to running drugs and settled in the first place he could find for her to give birth: Aruba.

When a U.S. citizen gives birth abroad, the child inherits the parents' citizenship, and all they have to do is notify the nearest embassy or consulate to record the birth and receive paperwork recognizing the citizenship of the child. My mother had become a naturalized U.S. citizen in 1972 (Dad never was anything but an Argentine and for all intents and purposes an illegal immigrant).

Dad ran drugs and was a wanted man and Mom a known associate, so they never went anywhere near the U.S. government to report my birth. A few months after I arrived in the world, she flew in a small aircraft to Miami and smuggled me into the United States.

Because of my parents' actions, and inactions, I had no status and was considered an illegal immigrant.

Another fact I learned from Mom: she only received food stamps and other government assistance for having three children, not four.

On the next call from Dad, I told him I knew about my citizenship. He said, "So what? What does that have to do with you getting a job?"

"Who's going to hire me?"

"Listen, you eat food that's for your little brother and sister."

I wanted to tell him about how Mom used their food stamps to get pills, but I remained silent.

When I said nothing more, he said, "You're fat and useless." He took a deep breath. "At your age I supported a family."

He'd done it by moving cocaine, but I didn't tell him that. I continued to be silent. Before he ended the call, he told me to man up, pound pavement, and find a job from strangers.

Not everyone in Miami paid income taxes. Most of the people I knew, like my mother, worked under the table. This practice of avoiding payroll taxes only occurred in small local businesses, and from what I had seen, these kinds of employers tended to mistreat their employees and generally paid shit.

I was insecure and didn't know how to negotiate this illegal arrangement with an employer. Mom had promised she'd help me get a job at her work, but her boss told her he didn't have any openings. I think he didn't want to hire an addict's kid.

I worried I'd be deported if I got caught, so I kept my head down and found work where and when I could. I moved furniture and occasionally picked up groceries at the bodega for my grandmother's neighbors. Every election cycle I got paid five bucks to stand on a street corner holding campaign signs for my friend's Republican father, even though I couldn't vote and getting rid of illegal immi-grants on welfare was one of the party's platforms.

None of this money was enough to get me away from home, so I spent it on coping mechanisms like D&D role-playing books and Magic: The Gathering cards.

I felt trapped. I went back to school. One day my marching band's drum major, Annie, appeared on the daily homeroom news broadcast with an announcement. She said that there were legal services that had helped her and students like her achieve legal immigration status and that a law firm provided such services for free. I kept a straight face and watched for reactions in the class, but no one paid any attention.

I never talked to Annie, and I hadn't known she too was here ille-gally. I had my head so far up my own ass, I never thought to consider I wasn't the only one. Here was Annie on the school's internal TV system, telling everyone she was an illegal in a school that called us "refees," "rafters," "wetbacks," and worse. I wouldn't have told anyone in the school, and because of the color of my skin, no one suspected I was one. Annie was different; she was brave. I never told her.

I wrote down the number for the law office and later that afternoon called and made an appointment that week with one of the lawyers.

The law offices were located in downtown Miami, so after school I took a thirty-minute bus ride from my grandmother's apartment.

The small office building had an unattended lobby. A wall-mounted placard with the names and numbers of occupants listed the immigration law firm on the third floor.

The office was by the elevator. I expected it to be bigger, but it looked like a closet with a window. A small white woman in a nice business suit sat surrounded by file folders. Her desk took up most of the office, and the computer monitor was too large. The door was open, but I gave it a timid knock.

I had to swallow a few times to find my voice. "Hi. I think I have an appointment with a lawyer? My name is Aramís." I never went by my nickname outside of home.

"Yes." A big smile appeared on her face. "My name is Lisa. I'm the lawyer you spoke to on the phone." She stood and stretched out her hand.

I hesitated. I wasn't sure if I should give her a firm handshake like my father had taught me or a gentle one since she was a woman. I decided to go with the former, and she had a strong grip. She gestured to the chair by the door and we sat.

Lisa grabbed one of the files on her desk—I don't know how she knew which one was mine—and opened it to review the information I had given over the phone. "Okay, Aramís, what brings you here?"

I wiped my hands on my jeans. "I don't have a Social Security number, and my mom says I don't have legal status. I want to work and, you know, be legal."

She grabbed a pen and scribbled on the paperwork. "Okay, let's go through some basic information. So you're fifteen, born in Aruba, and have been in the United States since you were three months old. Is that correct?"

My knee bounced, and I wish I'd brought something to hold, just to keep my hands busy. "That's right."

She wrote something on the margin of the intake form. "Okay, and your parents are also Aruban?"

"No."

She scribbled more. "Okay, let's start with mom. What's her citizenship?"

"She's American. I mean, she was born in Cuba, but she's been here since she was six, I think." I stared at the succulent plant on her windowsill and tried to figure out if it was real or fake.

"When did she get naturalized?"

"I don't know. Before I was born." The plant had a shade of green that looked too vibrant, but the details on the leaves were really good.

Lisa looked up. "And is Dad Cuban and naturalized?"

I laughed and she raised her eyebrow. I wiped my lips to hide the grin on my face. "Oh, no, definitely not. He's an Argentine, and, uh, I don't think he's legal."

She went back to her notes. "Do you have siblings?"

"Yes, three younger. And I have two older half brothers, but one died when I was two and . . ." I stopped. There was so much information in my head, and I didn't know how to best communicate it to her or anyone. Between my ears I had much to tell and many stories, most of them fiction but all of which explained everything I was. But who the fuck would believe?

She nodded in a way that was slow, and I think she was trying to say *sorry to hear that*. She continued, "What is their immigration status?"

"They are all American." I lifted my shoes to look at the bald treads and the hole in the right sole.

She put down her notes, placed the pen on the desk, and closed the file. Her smile had disappeared, and she started stroking her chin. "How did that happen?"

I told her what I knew. She kept a straight face the entire time.

When I finished, Lisa tapped her chin and leaned back in her chair. "There are two ways we can do this. We can apply for your citizenship through the INS based on your immediate family's status."

I sat up straight. "Oh, then I'm good? I can work?"

"Well, no. Basically it will take up to five years and maybe longer to get approved. You'd have to go with your mother every few months for interviews and renew a visa every year. To work legally you'd need a permit, and that can take a while to get approved."

I didn't want to be in a position to have to depend on Mom, not anymore. "Ah. You said two ways?"

"Yes," she smiled. "This other way is better. See, you've always been an American citizen. You mother just didn't notify the U.S.

embassy and get you a passport when you were born. So all you have to do is apply for a U.S. passport, and all they need is proof she was a U.S. citizen at the time of your birth and your birth certificate stating she is your mother. Easy."

"Wow. That is easy. What do I have to do?"

She grabbed a yellow notepad and wrote down a list. "I have the form here, but you'll need to take a picture. There are plenty of places that do them." She wrote the names of some businesses that provide passport photos. "A certified true copy of your mother's naturalization certificate and your birth certificate translated into English."

"Where do I get certified true copies?"

"You can go to the Miami–Dade County clerk of court and request it." She wrote the address of the office.

"Do I need my mom to come?"

Lisa considered the question for a moment. "No, it's public record. It's recorded in the official record book. Just pay twenty dollars or so." She paused again. "If you need help paying for that, I can help."

"What about my birth certificate?"

"Oh, we can find someone to translate." She tore the yellow sheet and handed it to me, like giving me a D&D quest.

Her handwriting was neat, and it struck me as beautiful. "No, how do I get a certified true copy?"

She started to put my file in a stack behind her on the floor. "You don't have your birth certificate?"

I shook my head. "Only a copy. And it's in Dutch."

Lisa shrugged. "Well, no problem. You'll have to contact their consulate and request it."

"Okay." I had a path with a destination. I believed all I had to do was complete the tasks on this list and I'd achieve my goals.

The next day I called the county clerk of court's office. Mom's naturalization certificate cost twenty-five dollars. The nearest place that did passport photos charged eight bucks. Mom had already spent her paycheck and told me to wait for next payday. I didn't want to ask Lisa for the money because I hated the idea of asking a stranger for help. I told Alle what I needed to do to get my citizenship squared away, and she scrounged up enough for me to pay the fee and take the passport photo. I relied on her more than I should've. She lived on Social Security, from check to check, and Abo was getting worse, but she never turned me away, and she always gave me as much as I needed.

Within a week of meeting Lisa, I'd paid the fees, filled out forms, and gotten my passport picture. I grew more confident and felt my life was making progress for the first time in years, and every item crossed out on the list Lisa had written was a mountain I'd climbed. All my hopes were stuffed in a manila envelope and ready to be sent to a U.S. passport agency, but my birth certificate was another matter.

Aruba had gained its independence from the Netherlands in 1986, five years after I'd been born. The Netherlands still handled diplomacy for the island nation, and my calls to their consulate had been met with long holds and indifferent bureaucrats. They said they'd forward my request to the proper department, but I never heard from any official.

My father's phone calls had gone from weekly to monthly and had shrunk to a few minutes long. Our relationship had become strained since I'd voiced my objections to Islamic scholars and he'd expressed his disapproval of my friends and hobbies.

After the usual greetings in Arabic, I told him about Lisa. He didn't allow me to finish telling him the plan. "No, scrap that, son. You need to get your Dutch citizenship instead."

"What? I don't even speak Dutch."

"You'll learn it. Doesn't matter. The United States is corrupt, satanic, and due for a collapse. When 5/5/2000 happens, you'll see." Dad took a deep breath.

"But . . ."

"If you can get a dual citizenship, that's better."

"I . . ."

"Call the Dutch consulate again and tell them you are a citizen. This is important, Peté." A corrections officer spoke in the background. "I gotta go. Do this, it's better. I love you." The line went dead.

I did as he said. I called the Dutch consulate and told them I should be a citizen and needed to know how to procure proof. A bored man on the other end of the line explained in bad English that citizenship in the Netherlands didn't work the way it did in the United States. My parents, or at least one of them, had to be Dutch or I had to have lived in a Dutch territory for five years. I thanked him and he hung up. I didn't want to be Dutch anyway.

My efforts to get my U.S. citizenship formalized had stalled. I met with Lisa a couple of times in the following months to ask for her help, but she had as much luck as I had. It seemed impossible to move forward anymore, and I sank.

At the bottom I'd started to become restless again. I kept sneaking out at night, and sometimes I slept on the beach or a park bench, but mostly I kept moving. As long as I moved, I could daydream, think, and hope. To lie still was terrible. I'd come home with the sunrise and stink of the street.

I slept at my grandparents' apartment on some of these mornings. Alle tucked me in and whispered hopes: *Believe tomorrow will be better and it will be. Sleep and dream good things so they come true. You're a good boy and good will come to you one day.*

Later, I dropped out of school again. At sixteen, I was still a freshman.

12

Mom stopped coming home a few months after I turned sixteen. She'd moved in with an old man who lived in my grandparents' building. His name was Leo, and the first time I met him he smiled and told me he had been a Marine in Vietnam. I found out he was HIV positive and had a lot of the pills Mom loved.

Memé had come back—wholly addicted to opioid pills. She'd also come out as a lesbian, though in our family it hardly made any waves; our grandmother shrugged, Mom laughed, and Dad mused about how much she was like him. Our relationship continued to fall apart, and we fought like we had as small children, except this time I'd hit back. Puberty had made me strong, so Memé started resorting to knives. I'd be forced to lock myself behind the nearest door. After Mom ditched us, Memé left Alle's apartment to live with another older woman who supplied her with pills. She never lived with family on a permanent basis again.

Uncle Sam continued to help Mom make ends meet with food stamps and welfare checks, even though Mom no longer lived with us and spent most of it on her needs. We continued to survive only because Alle kept us fed and housed. Some of the times it wasn't enough, and the electricity got cut for a few days or we had only their government cheese to eat.

The little ones, Peewee and Chiní, did the best they could among all this dysfunction. They spent most weekends with extended family and stayed safe after school with Alle and away from Mom and Memé.

I stayed out late with my nerd friends and slept on their couches.

I fell in love with a girl. She went to a different high school, but we had some nerd friends in common. We'd met at a Halloween party. I showed up wearing bits and pieces from a friend's Renaissance festival costumes. She came dressed as a hippie: blue hair, tie-dyed T-shirt and jeans, and a pretty smile. We both played flute and read books. She was smart, playful, and a dreamer. Her heart was twice as big as mine, and I loved holding her hand. She lived in a different part of Miami–Dade County, but I gladly walked any distance and rode buses or trains just to be with her.

My father teased me about puppy love and said I was young and intoxicated with horny teenager chemicals, but it didn't matter to me. Ultimately, he didn't approve of her because she was Catholic.

The older I got, the more Dad and I drifted apart. In the first few years after his capture, we had talked and planned about regrouping the family in Argentina. Questions kept popping up in my head, such as where we'd live. What school would I attend? What kind of work would Dad do? Would he go to prison there too? He didn't like to answer these, so I finally stopped asking.

I had wanted this dream of reuniting to become a reality, but as time moved along my father's goals and rhetoric got more fantastical. He grew more paranoid the longer he remained incarcerated. Years later, I'd find his doctor's scripts from prison pharmacies and see all the antipsychotics and antidepressants he was prescribed.

Dad blamed me for my inability to find steady work and fix my immigration status. I had told my closest friends and girlfriend the truth of my legal woes, and with their help I had begun to realize that the entire dilemma was my father's fault.

I stopped visiting and ignored his phone calls. My father continued to send me letters telling me to be prepared, to go with him to Argentina and ride out the apocalypse with him, but I didn't want to leave anymore.

I still have the last letter of his that I read:

In the name of Allah, The Most Gracious and The Most Merciful

Dearest Peté,

As-salamu-aliakum-wa-rahmatullahi-wa-barakatu, son. Today I finished a legal job and I'm going to send you two-hundred dollars in an envelope with your name on it. I don't know if this money will arrive before or after the other money from my sister sent to Memé, none the less: get your boots with whichever one gets there first, OK? And send me the rest of the money or the whole of it (if you buy your boots from my sister's check) because I'll be broke after my next phone call and I don't like to be mute.

I haven't been asking about your prayers . . . how are they doing? I would like to know if you ever actually finished a complete reading of the whole Holy Quran (and all footnotes) as we said you were. I tried very hard, for years, to be able to get you that copy of the good translation and the dictionary for you to enter the gate, to have the best access to this knowledge of fundamental truth . . . did you benefit from my struggle? You said yesterday some more about "my future activities" and I wonder, I think and ponder . . . does he understand "life" enough to question what will I do or . . . does he know me to such a small degree that he has to keep on asking me . . . or doesn't he know in his heart that I will do whatever is necessary for our survival! Whatever it takes: regardless of risks . . . yes! Rob banks, kill, maim . . . whatever! I'm not going to eat of my grandmother's social security checks nor of my mother and sister's and little brother's welfare check: I won't do that!

How does that grab you? Between you and me Peté, let's come to a serious agreement: until such a day when you learn what it is to support yourself, to provide for your shelter, clothing, food, transportation, etc. (each and every need, including organic ones) do not ask again, trying to approve or disapprove what I would or would not do to gain my livelihood (which probably would have to include yours, unless "something" big changes inside you.) There is something particularly wrong about my son who never earned a single day of his keep questioning: "Hey, what are you going to do for a living?" Like if I answered "wrong" (such as: smuggle dope!) then you wouldn't want any part of that . . . well let me ask you something Peté: what the fuck would you do if I don't earn your approval? I don't get the point of your question and I dislike your attempt at qualifying my means.

I understand that you might be worried about me getting caught again . . . is that it? I think we need to get this shit over with . . . we are very different and we should learn to live with that. You say you have a "conscience" that won't allow you to do wrong . . . deal drugs, or whatever "wrong" is to you. Very well. I have a conscience that would never and has never allowed me to be a parasite, a kept organism that needs a "host" to exist. Now what? Are you ashamed that I'm a drug dealer or a convicted one? I'm ashamed of thinking that I have a son that is six-four two-hundred-and-fifty pounds and has never worked a day in his life, lives with a poor grandmother and eats like he's supposed to be fed everyday . . . wakes up to no prayers, expecting breakfast and clothing to wear . . . thinks himself a man or damned close to it . . . never fought anyone his own size until bleeding or pain stopped the fight . . . thinks himself "man enough" to question his own father: how do you plan to make a living buster? And . . . doesn't see anything "wrong" with any of that!

And: I still love that son to fucking death. Are you with me? We're different in many, many ways . . . you've grown from the weirdest form of growing up . . . but the bottom

line Peté, is that you take me and throw me in China . . .
where I know nobody and I speak no Chinese and . . . we
know what will happen, right? I'll do what I've been doing
since I was fourteen years old: earn a living! Keep a wife, raise
children . . . yes! Go to prison too! OK? And we take you . . .
and put you to the test . . . that same test . . . maybe not
China, Miami? Buenos Aires? Why not Amsterdam or Aruba
maybe? You tell me what will happen Peté, when it's just you
and life . . . one on one, street no shelter of any kind . . . how
far do you think you will last? Do you ever think about this?
What happens in your thoughts when you do?

This is the difference between me and you. I'm a
survivor! I've engaged life under tremendously bad odds
and lived to tell the outcome of my struggle . . . you have
to learn to respect that . . . at least until the day when you
can show me: see! I went out and engaged in life, one on
one . . . further: I took a wife, raised children . . . fought hard,
took injuries and pain . . . and survived to come back to you
Dad . . . to show you that you don't have to deal drugs! But
until that day Peté, do both of us the favor of not ever, even
think that you have a "right" to disapprove or condemn my
way . . . my "wrongs" OK? Because that is so pathetically
ridiculous at this time as you can't even begin to understand.
For real: don't do that anymore. Fight a good fight! Get your
nose broken! Bust your knuckles and bleed all over a guy
much bigger than you . . . then come talk to me about what
I do "wrong." In the meantime and while all I ever hear you
fight is Memé . . . please do us a favor and let's talk about
other things.

I love you Peté and I want to help you become the best you
can be . . . but you're not letting me do anything . . . "somehow"
work, a job, to earn, to struggle, to fight doesn't enter in your
equation of life. Full belly, friends, activities . . . a girlfriend
phone call, school, music, band? These are your "factors," your
concerns . . . wow! Allah Akbar! He, the most beneficent alone
could allow you a place in His universe! I wouldn't!

If I was out there you'd have to work (hard work), earn your keep, help carry your weight son . . . fight by my side . . . you'd have to scrap with life, I would make you do all this and show me "conscience" and not talk about the shit . . . but I can't be there. So: I write you these letters that you don't answer . . . and I pray! And I wait. Patiently I wait for the day when the best of you will come to claim the whole of you . . . that day you'll be a "man." Today: you're my child and you assume wrongfully, that you can evaluate, as a man, your father's conduct or means to earn his livelihood . . . what an irony! Don't worry about your "future" too much. Live each day as if it was your last day . . . feel the difference in intensity of living like that and how you're doing it now. Try it! Trust me.

I send you all my love or whatever part of it you may understand . . . and insha Allah, I will forever remain, in this life and the next . . . in Shia Islam, your brother in truth, your very best friend and loving father.

Always!

Dad

Even today his last letter cuts me deep and breaks bones.

I dropped out my senior year. I turned eighteen, with no high school diploma and no citizenship. I worked handyman gigs, but I was stuck and had no future.

The U.S. government finally deported Dad to Argentina. I didn't even know he'd left until after it had happened. My family's disintegration was complete.

But I wasn't alone. I'd surrounded myself with friends, the ones my father had insulted: misfits, dreamers, nerds, idiots, and a thousand other names. My kind.

The next year my father's doomsday date of 5/5/2000 arrived and left. The world kept spinning.

Sometimes life bounces back from hopelessness, and self-destructive patterns rearrange themselves.

My mother's family finally recognized that my mother needed help. Her sister called the cops and used the Baker Act, a Florida law that allows the courts to commit a person to mental health treatment.

A miracle occurred: Mom found serenity and a chance to start over.

She had called me from the halfway house and wanted to see me again, maybe to work with her on the fourth step of recovery. I didn't recognize the woman she had become after sobriety: strong, disciplined, brave, compassionate.

Things got better after I reconciled with my mother. I enrolled at the local adult education center and completed the requirements for my high school diploma. I got a job at a gas station through my mother's contacts in Narcotics Anonymous and worked alongside people in recovery. They taught me about living one day at a time, and I began to understand life a little better.

The grandmother of the girl I'd fallen in love with had worked in embassies and consulates and spoke Dutch. She persuaded a Dutch clerk to provide her with a certified true copy and translation of my birth certificate. I sent my completed application to a U.S. passport agency and a year later proved my citizenship.

I enrolled in community college and moved back in with family to help my mom with bills and raising Chiní and Peewee. They did their homework and chores, Mom paid for after-school activities, and they did all the normal things teens experience that Memé and I never had. They grew up happy, I think.

I worked at night, went to classes in the morning, and took out college loans like everyone else my age. Then life took an unexpected turn.

September 11 happened, and I decided to enlist in the Marine Corps. Yes, I wanted to defend this republic, the country that had sheltered me and fed my family when they couldn't. Sure, I owed Uncle Sam a favor, but more specifically I believed something was missing in me and that I needed to prove myself.

My mother rarely spoke to Dad anymore. He had mocked her NA group and desire to be sober, but she'd called him in Argentina anyway and insisted I tell him about my decision to enlist. She supported my decision but wanted me to confront him and to make sure it was what I wanted to do.

He greeted me in the usual Islamic fashion, but I didn't play along anymore. Instead, I told him his doomsday book about May 5, 2000, was wrong. "Why did we ever believe it?"

He explained it away with "Allah's will." I could tell in his voice he was annoyed. Then I told him about joining the Marine Corps.

Dad got quiet and I thought maybe the call had dropped. Then he laughed and spoke to me like I was still eleven years old. "Son, you don't understand. You're not going to make it. You're putting your hand in the meat grinder."

"It's my hand."

Then he growled. "There's nothing in the Marines but faggots."

I don't know why he said that, but I ended the call. He had no power over me any longer; I was going to join the Marine Corps or die trying. We had gone our separate ways, but even though he no longer was a part of my life, his influence had long-lasting effects. A part of me, in a spot deep down where he had left marks, that spot believed I needed war to become stronger and more of a man. To become stronger than my father. Complete foolishness, but that is another story.

Four years later I became a father.

Dad called me at the naval hospital while I held my first daughter. My wife was the same teen girl I'd fallen in love with a lifetime ago.

My father still greeted me in Arabic. He congratulated us and we spoke briefly, but I had no interest in small talk.

Three years later I returned from my fourth Iraq deployment and met my second daughter for the first time. Being away from my children, especially missing my daughter's birth, greatly troubled me because it reminded me of my father being absent. Both Dad and I were kept away from our kids because of our line of work, regardless of the differences between our careers. And maybe just like my father, I had a hard time envisioning myself doing anything other than my profession.

Dad called again, like he'd been doing once every year at random times. I assumed Mom told him whenever I got back from Iraq. This time he wanted to tell me how proud he was of me and of what I'd accomplished in the Marines, and he begged for forgiveness. He wished he had been a better father, the kind I deserved.

I didn't know what to tell him, but I reasoned that if my mother had found serenity, why not him? Dad wanted to know me as a man, and so we talked, and I paced in the bedroom of our base housing in the dark.

I didn't ask what he was doing for money because I already knew, but it surprised me to learn he'd remarried and had a stepson.

"Do you treat him like all your sons?"

He laughed. "No, he couldn't handle it." I took that as his way of a compliment. He followed up, "He's a good kid, though."

"Lucky him."

Dad said, "I want to see you, but I can't go back to the States."

"I'm not going to Argentina. I have too much going on."

He hummed in understanding. "You need to hang up that uniform and be with your family."

I laughed. "You're a hypocrite, you know."

He sighed. "Yes. Yes, I know, and that's why I'm telling you to get out."

"I'm not done."

"Hm, okay."

He told me he loved me and ended the call. What he'd said about leaving the military made sense, but I wasn't ready to leave.

Two years later I had a son. We delivered him in our home, and it was the most powerful experience I'd ever had. I held him and thought of my father. He hadn't called in years, and I didn't have his number. I deployed overseas a month after my son's birth.

Months after I returned from deployment, I decided to reach out to Dad. Memé had his wife's number, and I called, asking for him in my atrophied Spanish.

She informed me in bad English that he'd had a series of strokes and she couldn't take care of him anymore. Dad lived in an assisted living facility, but she could take him home that weekend and we could do a video call so he could see all his grandchildren.

I saw him the following Saturday on my laptop screen. He'd gone gray and sat in a wheelchair, his posture bent and crooked. The stroke had robbed him of English, and the spark in his eyes had diminished. I didn't know what to say to him, so I presented to him his three grandchildren.

He looked at the camera confused, then his wife told him in Spanish that the people on the screen were his son and grandchildren.

He struggled to speak. "As-salamu-aliakum." Then he wept like a child.

Another five years had passed without hearing from him. It had become difficult for his wife to bring him home regularly on the weekends for calls; instead, she'd promised to keep in touch via Facebook.

Since our last call, Mom had died of cancer. I helped with her end-of-life care and sat by her side until the end. Her death hit me hard, and I grieved for years.

I left the Marine Corps a month after her death. I graduated college and started a career in IT but struggled to reintegrate into civilian life. I thought of how my father had said he couldn't do anything other than his profession and began to understand, but I was happier to watch my children grow and my marriage develop.

Then one day my father's wife called to say he'd died. She explained that he'd gone under anesthesia for an operation and had a stroke under the knife.

I felt nothing, as if I'd gotten the anesthesia instead of him. I'd accepted that my father had disappeared from my life long ago, but in truth I didn't know how to process the permanent nature of his death, and so his loss was trapped somewhere in my heart where I have no pain receptors. I'll never know anything more about him, and he'll never know me. I know only this: he died alone with no family or friends at his side.

My father trafficked drugs. He grew up in a family bereft of their patriarch and a misfit among his brothers and sisters. He'd been abused and abandoned and had to be in control to protect himself. Still, I make no excuses for him.

Dad had always tested me. My physical fitness, intelligence, and spirituality were under constant scrutiny, and most of the time he found me inadequate. He said he harmed me because he loved me and to prepare me for life and the impending apocalypse, to be ready for the bad times. He held me to a high standard, one that I never met.

I yearned for his approval and then later wanted to be nothing like him.

But I owe him gratitude for much more than just my existence. He encouraged me to read philosophy and literature and never let me get away with shit writing or meaningless spoken words. He taught me the meaning of fortitude and persevering through hardship.

I grew up and read his letters again, realizing that I write and talk as he did.

When I grow angry with my children, especially my son, I have to hold back the first words that come to mind because those are the same words Dad said to me, the same words I say to myself.

Sometimes I fail to hold myself back. I don't want my children to hear my voice, his voice, in their head. Instead, I want them to hear their own voices. They are better than I, better than my father.

Despite everything that happened with Dad, I want to believe that deep down inside of him beat the heart of a good man. I need to believe that someone like him can be redeemed, because that means any of us, even me, can become more than the sum of our mistakes.

He's been gone for years now, but I'm still keeping him alive. He exists in my memories of pain. His voice whispers in my head to stop being weak, useless, worthless.

When I became a father, he had told me he wished he'd been a better father. He said I had become as great as he believed I could be.

I often asked myself why he hadn't acted like the father I needed. I know the answer now: he was sick, an addict—a troubled soul. He loved me as best he knew how.

I forgive him so I can live but remember him to survive. I want him to finally have peace from a life lived always on the run. I need to grow up and cease being the little boy who wanted his father to be proud.

So, wherever you are Dad, rest easy. I know now I never needed to be anything other than who I am.

Milton Keynes UK
Ingram Content Group UK Ltd.
UKHW030336260924
448856UK00004B/85